Praise for *The Real-Time Revolution*

"As firms look to digitally transform their experience, Power and Ferratt provide a fascinating new lens to think about transformation—the role of time. I am sure their book will be highly influential."

—**Munir Mandviwalla, Executive Director, Institute for Business and Information Technology, Temple University**

"If you are a business leader seeking to keep up with the transformational power of technology to cope with the increasing demands of the environment and build an enterprise that can cope with rapid change, I urge you to read this book. This book will show you how to engage your customers and empower your employees so that you can join and lead the real-time revolution. A must-read!"

—**Andrew H. Schwarz, Professor, Stephenson Department of Entrepreneurship & Information Systems, Louisiana State University**

"Jerry Power and Tom Ferratt have come up with a perspective on time and how it is viewed by customers that can raise useful questions relative to one's own products and services. Their perspective emphasizes both the value of shortening duration as well as adding valued engagement while structuring interactions between organization and customer. I found it stimulating to apply these concepts to the enterprises where I am a participant."

—**Fred Niederman, Shaughnessy Endowed Professor, Saint Louis University**

"In an era in which real-time response capabilities are increasingly essential for an organization's digital transformation, this book is required reading for leaders who want to understand the levers that help organizations fully embrace the value of customer time."

—**Alexander Benlian, Professor and Dean, Darmstadt University of Technology, Germany**

"If you are a business owner or a leader who has been baffled with how to differentiate in today's digital world, this book helps unpack the mystery. Customers are looking for faster and easier, but we also need to recognize the individual needs and preferences of those customers. This book brings a practical approach to valuing your customers' most important resource—time—recognizing that responsiveness and 'real-time' expectations continue to evolve."

—**Mary Marcus, PhD, founder and Chief Innovator, OrganizationDynamic Inc.**

"'Time is of the essence' has held true for many years. This book highlights the urgent need to value our customers' time. Highly relevant and action oriented, it is a must-read for all leaders striving to stay competitive in today's market-place."

—**Lynn Mangan, President, Clubessential**

"In this original and important work, Power and Ferratt explain the significance of firms being able to leverage ongoing real-time relationships with customers and thereby improve the quality of customer time. This is not just a matter of being fast. In a nuanced and practical fashion—armed with diverse examples—the book identifies a set of competencies required for capturing real-time advantage."

—Mel Horwitch, former University Professor, Central European University (CEU), and former Dean, CEU Business School

"Technology advancements are pushing the envelope of time management. As our digital world continues to rapidly advance, this book is essential for anyone associated with information or transformational technologies!"

—Steve Garske, PhD, Senior Vice President and Chief Information Officer, Children's Hospital Los Angeles

"*The Real-Time Revolution* is both progressive and practical. Innovation is no longer enough. In a digital age, organizations must compete for consumer time and align their operations to do so. This book is a playbook for Digital 2.0."

—Ted Ross, CIO, City of Los Angeles

"Time has become the currency of our lives. Power and Ferratt explore time as a customer-centric value for businesses. They persuasively argue—with real-world, real-time case studies across industries—that valuing customers' time is *the* key battleground and marketplace differentiator. They provide a new framework for real-time organizations—those that value time from the perspective of the customer—which will deliver a better customer experience and greater success."

—Heidi Taylor, Managing Director, Heidi Taylor Marketing, and author of *B2B Marketing Strategy*

"This book explains a paradigm shift that is impacting all business sectors as organizations transform themselves to place increased attention on the customer experience. Power and Ferratt challenge you to think across boundaries, both within and outside an organization. The real-time monitoring and response process provides a good tool for producing benefits using technologies like IoT. I highly recommend this book."

—Vivek Chhabra, founder of 21iQLabs and former Vice President and General Manager, Mobile and Cellular IoT Business, Marvell

"One of the time-tested aphorisms in the business world speaks to the 'time value of money.' In *The Real-Time Revolution*, the focus is more on the 'money value of time.' Time may be money, but speed is profit: digital transformation is here, and the sooner companies embrace its inexorable impact, the sooner they will reap the benefits, as laid out in *The Real-Time Revolution*."

—Steven Shepard, PhD, founder of Shepard Communications Group, LLC, and author

"In an industry where quality-of-experience and quality-of-service are metrics for key progress indicators, Power and Ferratt highlight the urgency of transforming to a real-time company to meet and anticipate the needs of the customer. As we anticipate the fourth industrial revolution, the book is an invaluable testament to the importance of time as a key market differentiator."

—Ralf Jacob, President, Verizon Digital Media Services

The Real-Time Revolution

The Real-Time Revolution

Transforming Your Organization to Value Customer Time

Jerry Power and Tom Ferratt

Forewords by
Jim Ellis and John Mittelstaedt

Berrett–Koehler Publishers, Inc.

Berrett-Koehler Publishers, Inc.
1333 Broadway, Suite 1000
Oakland, CA 94612-1921
Tel: (510) 817-2277
Fax: (510) 817-2278
www.bkconnection.com

ORDERING INFORMATION

Quantity sales. Special discounts are available on quantity purchases by corporations, associations, and others. For details, contact the "Special Sales Department" at the Berrett-Koehler address above.

Individual sales. Berrett-Koehler publications are available through most bookstores. They can also be ordered directly from Berrett-Koehler: Tel: (800) 929-2929; Fax: (802) 864-7626; www.bkconnection.com.

Orders for college textbook / course adoption use. Please contact Berrett-Koehler: Tel: (800) 929-2929; Fax: (802) 864-7626.

Distributed to the U.S. trade and internationally by Penguin Random House Publisher Services.

Berrett-Koehler and the BK logo are registered trademarks of Berrett-Koehler Publishers, Inc.

Printed in the United States of America

Berrett-Koehler books are printed on long-lasting acid-free paper. When it is available, we choose paper that has been manufactured by environmentally responsible processes. These may include using trees grown in sustainable forests, incorporating recycled paper, minimizing chlorine in bleaching, or recycling the energy produced at the paper mill.

Library of Congress Cataloging-in-Publication Data

Names: Power, Jerry, author. | Ferratt, Thomas W., author.
  Title: The real-time revolution : transforming your organization to value customer time / Jerry Power and Tom Ferratt.
  Description: First edition. | Oakland, CA : Berrett-Koehler Publishers, Inc., [2019] | Includes bibliographical references and index.
  Identifiers: LCCN 2019015428 | ISBN 9781523085637 (hardcover)
  Subjects: LCSH: Time management. | Customer relations. | Organizational change.
  Classification: LCC HD69.T54 P67 2019 | DDC 658.8/12--dc23
  LC record available at https://lccn.loc.gov/2019015428

First Edition

24 23 22 21 20 19   10 9 8 7 6 5 4 3 2 1

Interior design and production: Dovetail Publishing Services
Jacket design: Adam Johnson

We sincerely thank our wives, Jean Power and Debbie Ferratt, for their assistance, encouragement, understanding, and most of all the love they shared with us as we devoted our time to writing this book.

Jerry Power and Tom Ferratt

Contents

Foreword

by Jim Ellis

*Dean of the Marshall School of Business,
University of Southern California*

Jerry Power and Tom Ferratt address in a head-on manner the scarcest resource we have—that of time—in every aspect of business. Advances in technology have allowed businesses to become more efficient and they have made markets more competitive. The next frontier for businesses has to place much more emphasis on the efficiencies we bring to customers with the products and services we provide. The examples they use from many diversified sectors are significant in that they show how the issue of time can be addressed successfully. The book is extremely practical, a thoughtful read, and one that anyone doing business with anyone else must read.

In the past, inventory, quality, and pricing were chief differentiators in success. The increased use of data sets pushes the envelop further by allowing companies to become more anticipatory rather than reactive. This book addresses the differentiator of customer time, the final logical piece of the puzzle. The consumers of today know they have a finite number of minutes in their day, and they want to maximize those—this book gives organizations ways to up their game in order to save customers time when buying and using their products and services. The authors have created an outstanding template for us to think about how we serve the market faster. It is a game changer of thought, as it truly makes you think.

Jim Ellis
Dean of the Marshall School of Business
University of Southern California

Foreword

by John Mittelstaedt

Dean of the School of Business Administration,
University of Dayton

Last year for his birthday, I ordered a custom-made tie for my father. Neckties from small high schools in South Dakota are not commonly available in stores in Ohio, or anywhere else for that matter. I designed the tie and then paid extra at checkout for two-day shipping. I was more than willing to pay a little more to ensure I could see the excitement in my father's eyes. The website was clear that I could speed delivery for an additional charge; what was not clear was that it would take eighteen days to make the tie. At that point fast delivery lost its meaning.

A late gift for one holiday does not represent a crisis. But, though this story is unique, it is far from uncommon. In my industry, students make educational decisions based on how quickly we read their applications and how quickly we respond to their questions. Our ability, or inability, to respond in real time begins to form their opinions of how we will treat them as students. The ability to recognize the real-time value of satisfying customers' time-related needs is both a challenge and an opportunity for any organization. Jerry Power and Tom Ferratt see it as a revolution in the making.

Firms recognize that customers value time, but they struggle to capitalize on the opportunity it presents. For years, we have understood time as an organizational cost to be controlled, but we have not always seen the value of time from the perspective of the end user. This book recognizes that the ability to value customer time has become a differentiating advantage. It recognizes that thinking of time as a value to customers is different from thinking about time as a cost to be managed. Customers don't care what it costs you to make and deliver a product or service. They care that it serves a need, and in in our world, timing is a critical part of the need.

The good news is that *The Real-Time Revolution* offers companies and executives a framework and road map for making time a real competitive advantage. Through a nuanced understanding of theory and research and the use of numerous examples, Power and Ferratt build your tool kit for increasing your organization's agility in detecting and responding to changing customer expectations regarding the value of time. Moreover, building your organization around the value of real time gives you ways to treat your own people better, thereby making your organization a better employer.

John Mittelstaedt
Dean of the School of Business Administration
University of Dayton

Preface

Time is a precious commodity. In a world where the pace of business is continually accelerating, time is becoming the dominant customer currency. Customers want to spend their scarce time well. For example, when ordering a product, the ideal ordering process from the customer's perspective would take virtually no time and would be completed effectively. The order would be accurate and complete so the customer can avoid spending time on corrective actions.

Real time in this ordering example is the actual time that a customer has to invest with a company to complete the ordering process. However, completing an order (or any process) in "real time" has popularly come to mean completing it virtually instantaneously. The reality is that instantaneous order handling may not always be possible. It is an ideal to strive to achieve, but in reality a rushed delivery of the wrong product or a product that is hard to use will ultimately prove to be counterproductive. From the customer's perspective, ideal customer experiences include a chain of events that, in their totality, are completed effectively and as instantaneously as possible.

Organizations striving to continually improve their ability to provide ideal customer experiences are real-time organizations. They are the core of what we call "the real-time revolution." These organizations are demonstrating to the customer that they value the customer's time. Organizations that come closer than their competitors to this ideal will begin to be viewed as the customer's preferred provider. As real-time companies distance themselves from their competitors, they will begin to gain market share. Companies that are unable to match the competition's efforts will be forced to offset their deficiencies by reducing prices and margins. Use of financial incentives may serve as a temporary means to maintain market position. However, if the company is in real-time denial, the ultimate survival of the enterprise will be threatened by other organizations that embrace the real-time revolution.

Organizational leaders have to ask themselves a critical question: "Does our organization truly recognize the importance of time to customers?" What may seem like a simple question requires significant effort to develop the data needed to provide the answer honestly and completely. For example, those in leadership positions will need to consider where and how their customers spend time dealing with the company and its products over the life of the products and services. In addition, they must be able to prioritize their constrained resources so that efforts to improve the customer experience are optimally targeted to projects that customers appreciate. We cite numerous examples throughout the book that show how companies have used real-time concepts to provide meaningful improvements to customer experiences.

This book is for the leaders and members of organizations seeking to understand how they can help make their organizations more "real time." That includes those in organizations that are just starting to focus on valuing customer time, those in organizations that have implemented some programs to improve customer experiences and are looking to do more, and those who feel threatened by competitors that have been able to win market share by improving their efforts to value customer time. We wrote this book to help all of these readers understand better how to transform their organizations to become more real time.

The book is also for leaders and members of organizations in real-time denial. They may not realize their dire condition. If they continue to ignore the migration of customers to competitors that are providing better real-time experiences, their customer base will eventually disappear. The real-time revolution will leave them wondering why their customers abandoned them. Hopefully this book will help them realize their need for transformation so they can survive and even thrive.

The book is organized to help readers first understand the importance of the real-time revolution and the need to become a real-time organization (introduction and chapter 1). We then explain why leaders need to establish a real-time monitoring and response (RTMR) system to track and adapt to ever more demanding customer expectations about time (chapter 2). The remainder of the book helps readers understand various levers available to transform their organizations to provide customers with experiences that value their time throughout the life of their organization's products and services. These include the core levers of the product or service (chapter 4), processes (chapter 5), data (chapter 6), and people (chapter 7). Beyond those core levers are technology, culture, strategy, and relationships with a variety of external parties (chapter 8).

The message throughout the book is straightforward: to survive and thrive, organizational leaders, in concert with their members and other stakeholders, must transform their organizations to value customer time more effectively than competitors do. Three related guidelines support this transformation to real time:

1. The real-time organization must be agile enough to detect and respond to changing customer expectations regarding time better than competitors do.

2. The real-time organization must engage customers throughout the life of its products and services such that customers view the organization as valuing their time and, thus, meeting their needs more than competitors do.

3. The real-time organization will be transformed to value customer time through these core organizational levers: products and services, processes, data, and people.

This message applies not only to businesses but also to other organizations where customer real-time expectations are important to meet, including governmental entities, educational institutions, and other not-for-profits. The message is of equal or even greater value for readers in educational institutions that are preparing future organizational leaders to guide their enterprises to success in an increasingly turbulent world. These participants could be students in degree programs (such as graduate programs in business, public, or educational administration) or non-degree programs (such as learning/leadership development programs offered by a specific organization or a professional association).

As the examples throughout the book illustrate, the most successful organizations have recognized that time is increasingly important to customers. One of our contributions from observing these organizations is recognizing that what began as a collection of independent efforts has become a larger movement, a real-time revolution. Organizations around the world are striving to meet customer time expectations. As a result, they are changing the basis for competitive success and failure. Our research indicates that even though most companies are striving to take advantage of digital technologies, those focusing on transformations that customers see as valuing their time have the best bottom-line impacts. Our other contribution is the set of three related guidelines above to assist organizational leaders, members, change agents, and other stakeholders in spreading the message of the real-time revolution: transform your organization to value customer time.

Real Time and the Real-Time Revolution

Ryan Clark of Liberty Bottleworks runs a small plant that makes aluminum drinking bottles. Liberty customers can customize their products online to the exact shape, size, color, and graphic of their choice. Through lean manufacturing, just-in-time inventory, and digital technologies, "we can turn on a dime. We can do customized manufacturing simply and easily," Clark says. Instead of having to make ten thousand bottles to make a profit, "I can do ten, with the specifications beamed straight from the art department or straight from the customer." These capabilities for producing customized drinking bottles give this small shop a strong edge over its mass-producing competition.[1] One manifestation of that competitive edge is found in the real-time online interface to the production process. The ease with which customers can enter customized production requirements tangibly demonstrates that Liberty Bottleworks values its customers' time in completing this process more effectively than competitors do. The faster production demonstrates further the value that Liberty Bottleworks places on time not only for its own benefit but also for its customers.

A growing number of organizational leaders are paying attention to the increasing value that customers are placing on their time. Time is becoming the dominant customer currency. For many interactions with an organization and its products and services, customers would prefer to minimize the expenditure of their scarce time. For example, customers of Liberty Bottleworks would prefer to minimize the time spent customizing product design and placing an order. If they must spend time, they would prefer it to be easy, convenient, and fast. Leaders of Liberty Bottleworks have paid attention. They have transformed processes to make them easier, more convenient, and faster for their customers. When organizations make such transformations, they are valuing customer time more than they did previously.

The actual time for Liberty Bottleworks' customers to customize product design and place an order is the real time for completing those processes. Although the actual time is the real time for these events, "real time" has come to mean instantaneous.[2] Given the customer desire to spend as little time as possible on these processes, the ideal time for these processes would be instantaneous. In addition, these processes would be completed effectively. That means the specifications and order would be complete and accurate. Incomplete or inaccurate orders and specifications would lead to spending additional time to make corrections. To be ideal real-time customer experiences, the experiences should be instantaneous and effective.

Part of Liberty Bottleworks' design-ordering-production process is now instantaneous and effective. The data from the design and ordering processes flow directly to the production process. The order and the design specifications go instantaneously to manufacturing through an online interface between the customer and manufacturing. There is no waiting for someone to process the order.

On a continuum of effective real-time customer experiences, instantaneous is at one end. Submitting an order with production specifications to manufacturing and receiving immediate confirmation would place Liberty Bottleworks at that end. Longer actual experiences would be placed farther from that end. As companies undergo transformations, they often strive to reduce the time of these longer experiences.

Places could be marked on the continuum to compare customer time prior to a transformation and after a transformation. Customizing product design at Liberty Bottleworks may have previously taken four hours for customers to meet with an artist and walk through various choices. After transformation, it may take fifteen minutes to click through various choices without needing to meet with an artist. In addition to comparing those marks, Liberty Bottleworks would also want to compare the marks showing their time to customize product design with the competition's time.

Leaders may find it helpful to post graphs of customer experiences before and after a transformation. Such graphs could show the time of various customer experiences across the life of each affected product and service. These end-to-end graphs would include customer experiences, as applicable, from initial design through use, maintenance, and disposition. The graphs would show the organization's progress toward becoming a more real-time organization if actual time for customer experiences after transformation were closer to the more instantaneous end of the graph.

In an effort to accelerate one customer-facing process, some companies have found that other customer-facing processes have become extended. Consider a company that reduced product testing time only to discover that customer support processes increased as a result. This would be an example of an ineffective effort to make the company more real time and should be visible on an end-to-end graph.

Instantaneously effective real-time customer experiences are at the core of the real-time revolution. Companies striving to provide ideal real-time customer experiences are driving the real-time revolution. They may not currently provide customers with instantaneously effective experiences, but they are focused on that objective. The closer they get to the goal, the more real time they become. Companies that are more real time than their competition are the ones that will survive and thrive.

We live in an increasingly competitive world where business survival requires valuing what customers value. Though the internet has opened the door to a wealth of new business opportunities, that same door encourages competitors to win customers away from other businesses. Customers will always be looking for great products, and companies will always be striving to make potential customers aware of their offerings. Geographic and information barriers are dissolving. That increases the number of competitors fighting for the same customers. In such competitive markets, customers prefer to buy from companies they trust to share their values. Placing a high priority on the value of their time is emerging as a critical value that customers are expecting companies to demonstrate. Although the value of time is not the same for everyone, everyone can agree that time is a finite resource that should not be wasted. When customers are comparing offers from different competitive suppliers, the company that demonstrates a respect for the customer's use of time also demonstrates a shared sense of value that will increase the trust between customer and supplier.

For some organizational leaders, valuing customer time is an extension of their traditional efforts to become more competitive. For example, their existing plans and projects may focus on optimizing operational efficiencies, becoming more agile, executing a digital transformation, or improving customer experiences. These leaders need to shift their view of the value of time from an internal organizational perspective to the customer's perspective. For some of these leaders, valuing customer time will be a revolutionary approach to business, perhaps even an opportunity to leapfrog the existing competition and redefine market expectations. All leaders—whether chief executive officers (CEOs); other C-level executives such as chief marketing officers (CMOs), chief financial officers (CFOs), chief operating officers (COO), and chief information officers (CIOs); or leaders at any level who are responsible for leading a change effort—should consider a fundamental question: "Will using the customer's value-of-time lens lead to reshaping my view of the business and its competitive environment?"

As a core principle, organizational leaders, in concert with their members and other stakeholders, must transform their organizations to value customer time more effectively than competitors do. Research has shown that real-time organizations are growing faster than industry averages (see Exhibit 1.1);[3] furthermore, valuing customer time is a defining characteristic for real-time organizations. As discussed with the Liberty Bottleworks example, valuing customer time means investing a company's resources to minimize the expenditure of the customer's scarce time for many experiences. That means providing effective experiences that are faster than customers expect.

A fast but not fully effective experience could have negative repercussions. For example, consider a customer unloading bags after a fast trip to buy twelve bags of mulch, which were loaded by store employees, only to discover eleven bags in the vehicle. Now the customer has to make another trip to get the twelfth bag. Slightly slower but more complete order fulfillment would have created more value for the customer and avoided dissatisfaction with the store.

Speed is relative to the task at hand. For example, faster could mean seconds (e.g., when the interaction involves checking the status of an airline flight) or months (e.g., when the interaction involves the typical process of building a house). Thus, the speed of a real-time experience is not always instantaneous but is related to the process. In addition, it is also related to the capability of the competition, such as how long it takes other builders to complete a house.

Companies that save customers more time than competitors are effectively demonstrating, in a tangible way, that they respect them and appreciate the value of their time. In serving customers it is important to focus relentlessly on time in improving their experiences. The relentless focus on time applies to everyone and everything that contributes to competing successfully in serving customers, starting with the first

Selected chapters include guidance and insights inspired by one or more research projects sponsored by the Institute for Communication Technology Management (CTM) in the Marshall School of Business at the University of Southern California (USC) from 2015 to 2017. Research showing that real-time organizations are growing faster than industry averages comes from one of those projects, which was conducted by Omar El Sawy from USC and Pernille Rydén from Technical University of Denmark.

CTM is a USC Center of Excellence that is devoted to research and education to help the networked digital industry and its customers grow and prosper. The CTM consortium includes companies such as AT&T, CenturyLink, Children's Hospital, the City of Los Angeles, Fox, TDS, Telus, Verizon, and Warner Bros. CTM examines trends associated with networking, entertainment, consumer demand, and business services to better understand how technology impacts business process and markets as well as how business impacts the adoption of technologies.

Exhibit 1.1 USC Marshall Research Projects

time they are introduced to the company and continuing as long as they remain customers. This customer-centric view of time should be a driving force for interactions involving employees, subcontractors, supply chain and other support team members, as well as customers themselves, as they are involved in completing a process.

Historically, a company's focus on time translated to reducing the company's internal operational time. Less time translated to higher operational efficiencies, lower costs, and higher profits. In today's world, the internet has made businesses global. That has increased the competition as more businesses chase the same opportunities. With more competitors to choose from, customers have become more sophisticated in their selection process. They are looking for suppliers that can not only reduce costs through greater time efficiencies in their internal processes, but they are also looking for suppliers that can save them time. This is becoming especially true in a world where customers are increasingly multitasking and managing their personal lives on internet time. Examples of such recognition are seen in ease of ordering, rapid response of customer support, quality products that do not fail or need to be returned, and instructions that allow ease of use.

This new perspective on the value of time originates with the customer. From the customer's perspective, personal time is a precious resource. Improving the customer's experience vis-à-vis time is an end-to-end issue from the customer's perspective. It should become a similar issue from the perspective of companies seeking to win the customer's business. More specifically, a company wanting to improve its customers' time experience must assume that they start an "experience clock" when they first learn about or contribute to the design of a product or service. This experience clock continues to run through the time customers acquire the product, use it, service it, and achieve the desired level of satisfaction. Reducing the amount of time customers spend on a number of steps in the life of a product or service, such as ordering the product, configuring it for use, or disposing of it, is one way to improve their time experience.

The real-time clock is defined by an organization's customers. An organization's ability to participate in the real-time revolution can only be measured based on the customer's time experience. Customers develop expectations about the amount of time required to achieve a desired result. These real-time expectations are based on experiences with various products and services. These expectations reflect the baseline for the amount of time that a customer expects to invest when interacting with an organization. When the experience begins to extend beyond this baseline, the customer becomes open to alternative solutions that would move the time demand closer to expectations. When the experience is better than expected, the customer credits the company with the incremental value that can be achieved by reinvesting the newfound time savings.

Conversely, with a scarcity of time and an experience that is worse than expected, the customer attributes the opportunity cost associated with the lost time to the offending company. Consider the case when a customer is looking for a fast-food restaurant. For a modest investment of time there are certain expectations associated with the food, cost, and quality of the experience. If a competing restaurant can provide a similar dining experience in a shorter time period, the customer will consider the competitor as a more effective real-time restaurant.

For many products and services, the goal should be minimizing the expenditure of customer time while assuring that customer experiences are effective. However, there are also examples of customer experiences that are enjoyable, productive, or otherwise satisfying because of what the customer obtains. Improving the quality of time spent should be the goal of the organization for these customer experiences. Minimizing customer time in a movie theater is not the goal of a moviemaker; rather, it is to enhance the entertainment value of the customer's time spent. For the customer who wants a higher quality dining establishment, the main dining experience of eating a meal creates the most customer value. The quality of that experience needs to be maintained and improved. Nevertheless, the customer may perceive that faster subsidiary activities, such as making a reservation, getting seated, and paying the bill, enhance the main dining experience.

To illustrate, consider Cheesecake Factory's payment app, CakePay, designed to facilitate bill paying. Customers download the app, check into their specific dining location, and share their code with the server. They can then pay whenever they are ready without waiting for the server and without feeling rushed.[4] The use of a payment app such as CakePay supplements the main dining experience. Its intent is to demonstrate that the restaurant values customer time, particularly the time of repeat customers. It collects one-time information (e.g., name and credit card details) upon installation of the app rather than each time the customer pays. It gives the customer control over the time to pay. The mix of an excellent quality meal and fast, easy payment at a time of the customer's choosing results in a more enjoyable dining experience and, thus, a more valued customer experience.

Responding to an urgent customer need is another example of valuing customer time through improving the quality of time spent. Consider a customer who must present a printed report early the next morning. The customer's printer runs out of ink late in the evening before the report is due. After searching for a place to buy ink, the customer finds a not-so-convenient twenty-four-hour store that will respond to this urgent need. Even though the store is inconvenient, its ability to satisfy an urgent need improved the quality of the customer's experience, so the time spent to find and use this store becomes a positive investment.

Ultimately, valuing customer time means responding to customer time expectations more effectively than competitors do. Reducing the amount of time spent interacting with a company, its products, and its services is an appropriate way to demonstrate a company values its customers' time when they expect efficient interactions. In these instances, real-time organizations prioritize the pursuit of experiences that move the organization toward the instantaneously effective end of the real-time continuum. Alternatively, improving the quality of time spent is an appropriate way to value customers' time when they expect interactions with a company, its products, and its services to be enjoyable, productive, or otherwise satisfying.

A business must consider a whole range of activities that will affect its customers' perception of how the company values their time. Consider the case of Samsung and the Galaxy Note 7.[5] Samsung understood that the increased functionality of the smartphone was driving interest in devices with larger screens and improved performance. In order to respond rapidly to this evolving market, Samsung rushed the Note 7 to market with an inadequately tested battery. The result was that, under certain conditions, a cell phone might heat up and potentially catch on fire. Simply replacing the battery did not solve the problem because the replacement battery also had problems; thus, attempting to service the phone wasted customer time. Further, the phone had been widely distributed. By the time the problem was detected, the process to recall and replace the phone was protracted, further inconveniencing the customer.

So, while Samsung had the best of intentions in moving quickly to bring a technically advanced product to market, undetected flaws from rushed testing led to issues that undermined the value of the new product. Although the time to market was shorter, the time to service a flawed phone was too long, and a burning battery ignited a negative customer experience. To avoid similarly negative consequences, businesses should not focus on just one or two activities where they can trim time for specific processes. Instead, they must consider a whole range of activities affecting customer perceptions of how a company demonstrates that it values customer time. Those activities include the steps in the life of a product or service, from developing through producing to using the product or service. They include a broad range of activities for a business to consider as it seeks to transform itself and its products and services to value customer time better than competitors do.

The Real-Time Revolution

We are at the beginning of a revolutionary shift as an increasing number of individual leaders are undertaking projects within their companies to make them more real time. Most of these efforts would be best characterized as distinct and independent projects. As the scope increases and these projects become more frequent, the composite set of projects will need to be coordinated and orchestrated for maximal impact. Independent projects create an environment where individual departments seek to improve their own efficiencies. That risks redistributing time allocations within the organization without producing company-wide, customer-visible time-value improvements.

For organizations to survive and thrive, they must make valuing customer time—a precious as well as nonrenewable resource—their primary priority. When organizations adopt maximizing the value of customer time as a driving priority, they develop a North Star that can drive a series of coordinated business transformation projects. Such a guiding principle allows a real-time organization to continually engage customers more effectively than competitors do throughout the life of the organization's products and services. Managers of successful real-time transformations will change their products and services, processes, data, and people in order to continually improve their ability to value customer time more effectively than competitors. As competitors become better at valuing customer time through faster, more respectful, and more satisfying interactions with customers, the bar for what is "real time" will be raised, thereby raising customer expectations.

Over time, rising expectations mean that what was once considered real time is now slow. The former real time was considered fast, but what is now fast is closer to instantaneously effective. Competition will lead to a continuing cycle of rising customer expectations about what "real time" means. That will drive more organizations to seek to become more agile at detecting and responding to evolving real-time expectations.

The real-time revolution will accelerate as organizations begin to pursue more real-time transformational programs that require coordination between different functions. When multiple transformation projects are integrated and orchestrated to bring a much larger innovation to life, the benefits of transformations will begin to compound. Ultimately, companies will shift from thinking about real-time transformation programs as an effort to move from point A to point B to a situation where efforts to improve the customer's expenditure of time become a focal point for continual improvement. Valuing customer time is a continually moving target. Becoming a more real-time organization is a continuing journey rather than a destination.

Many organizations are currently undergoing pervasive, fundamental changes through digital transformations. Changing the way an organization conducts its business through innovative use of digital technologies focuses on such goals as offering new products, expanding markets, improving operational efficiencies, lowering costs, and increasing profits. Those transformation efforts are often missing the customer-centric focus of the real-time revolution. In contrast, the most successful business leaders in the real-time revolution undertake digital transformations with an overarching goal of valuing customer time. The value of time is emerging as the new competitive battleground. Leaders who fail to drive digital transformations in an atmosphere where valuing customer time is pervasive will eventually lose to those who embrace the real-time revolution.

Becoming more agile is another transformation organizations are currently pursuing. Some of these transformations have their roots in an effort to make software development teams more responsive to changing customer requirements. However, being agile has become important not only for software development but more broadly for project management and even more broadly for organizational management. In all of these situations, it is important to have the ability to monitor and evaluate relevant conditions and respond innovatively and effectively to changes in those conditions.

Being more agile is also important for becoming more real time. Major differences exist, though, between becoming more agile for a real-time organization and becoming more agile for software development, project management, and organizational management. These differences occur in the conditions that are monitored and the innovative responses to changes in those conditions. The real-time organization monitors and evaluates how it and its competitors value customer time. It also focuses on identifying and implementing innovative responses that value customer time more effectively than competitors do. Becoming more agile in the real-time revolution means that a real-time organization will continually monitor, evaluate, and respond to how it and its competitors value customer time. It will also seek to improve its effectiveness in doing so.

Transforming to a Real-Time Organization—Essential for Survival

Business leaders who do not transform their organizations to value customer time more effectively will find the survival of their organizations increasingly challenged as customers move to competitors that do. Not participating in the real-time revolution will lead to a withering customer base. A robust customer base that perceives that you respect them by valuing their time is essential for survival.

A real-time company is always striving to improve the customer's expenditure of time. Each step to improve this time expenditure will require some level of change within the company and, as a result, a real-time company has to embrace change as being a part of its DNA. Most people are inherently resistant to change. Thus, a barrier to participating in the real-time revolution is lack of interest or even resistance by others in the organization. These situations should be expected if employees are doubtful that change will bring a positive result for the company or if they think that change will negatively impact them. To overcome these potential barriers, it is often best to develop active participation and support of a critical core of employees. Persuade this core group to see the issue from the customer's perspective and to accept the transformation as a longevity issue for the company. They can serve as topical evangelists. They can help persuade others that the company's survival depends on pursuit of a real-time transformation. Developing this support is an important aspect of becoming a real-time revolutionary!

We present many examples of companies that are valuing customer time. They serve as signposts that indicate the real-time revolution is upon us. As a leader, expect that competitors are constantly pushing to make their companies increasingly real time. Set a target that gets ahead of the competition. Continue to strive to beat customer time expectations, whether those expectations arise from the competition or a self-established benchmark.

Demonstrating value for customer time is a primary driver of companies that have been convinced to join the real-time revolution. Nevertheless, those real-time organizations do not abandon traditional fundamentals of business. Real-time organizations must continue to pursue fundamental business goals of developing new products, expanding markets, improving operational efficiencies, lowering costs, and increasing profits. The guidance we provide in subsequent chapters is intended to provide an incremental focus on various levers that may be used to orchestrate changes that support becoming a more real-time organization. Those changes, though, should also be compatible with fundamental business goals.

The justification for a real-time transformation includes the conviction from an organization's leaders, members, and other stakeholders that to survive the organization must demonstrate that it values customer time more effectively than competitors do. It also includes a collective belief that customer time is the most precious resource guiding customer behavior; furthermore, failure to value that resource competitively will cause the organization's customer base to wither. This justification may be bolstered by how well a real-time transformation supports fundamental business goals. For example, a real-time transformation could involve a digital transformation that would allow the organization to get products to customers faster while also producing more in less time.

Beyond Survival

Leaders typically want their organizations not only to survive, but also to thrive. Surviving and thriving require succeeding in three different, but interrelated, areas:

1. Consistently demonstrating that the organization values customer time.

2. Monitoring how well the organization and its competitors value customer time and evaluating where to make improvements.

3. Continually identifying and implementing innovative improvements to demonstrate an ongoing commitment to improving customer time value more than competitors do.

We discuss each of these areas in the chapters that follow.

The skills required for each of these areas are quite different. The first area—consistently demonstrating that the organization values customer time—requires the mastery of repeatable procedures that allow for consistent performance. A number of organizational processes in this first area (e.g., production, delivery, and maintenance) involve actions and interactions with customers that make it possible to consistently demonstrate that the organization values customer time. Having the ability to work with these procedures to achieve traditional business goals of improving operational efficiencies, lowering costs, and increasing profits is also important to survive and thrive. The key distinction for a real-time organization is that the mastery of these skills must occur within the context of valuing customer time as a primary priority.

The skills for the second area—monitoring how well the organization and its competitors value customer time and evaluating where to make improvements—include the mastery of procedures that collect data. Moreover, evaluating where to make improvements includes data analysis and decision-making skills. The key distinction for a real-time organization is that the collection of data and subsequent analyses and decisions must take into account not only traditional business goals but also the overarching goal of valuing customer time. Without the overarching goal, the onrushing crush of real-time competitors will prevent thriving and surely threaten survival.

The third area—continually identifying and implementing innovative improvements to demonstrate an ongoing commitment to improving the value of customer time more than competitors do—is most challenging. Skills here include being innovative, managing change, and eventually institutionalizing innovations as routine procedures across a range of organizational functions. Having the ability to blend these skills while also achieving a variety of traditional business goals is also important to survive and thrive. Besides cost-control goals, traditional business goals include revenue-generating initiatives such as pursuing new or growth opportunities through new products or services, new market geographies, and new customers. The key distinction for a real-time organization is that the mastery of these skills must occur within the context of valuing customer time as a primary priority.

Our Urgent Message

Organizational leaders, in concert with organizational members and other stakeholders, must transform their organizations to value customer time more effectively than competitors do. As urgently as we can say it, our message is a matter of life and death for competitive business organizations.

Customers have an understanding of time that is different from the companies they buy from. Through experience, customers have developed expectations about how much time they are willing to invest in the companies they patronize; they have also developed expectations about the quality of that time, i.e., how satisfied they should be. These expectations have been shaped by previous experience with the company's competition and the company itself so that when a competitor offers a product or service that allows customers to personally become more efficient or satisfied, that competitor has an opportunity to gain mind and market share. Real-time organizations prioritize customer time and make sure that their efforts are a source of additional value for their customers. These organizations strive to become more real time. They strive to provide instantaneously effective customer experiences for activities that customers ideally expect to take none of their scarce resource of time. This striving is the distinguishing characteristic of a real-time organization.

We are at the beginning of a revolutionary shift toward more and more organizations transforming to become real time. As real-time competition increases and customers elect to abandon organizations that do not meet their real-time expectations, only those organizations that do meet real-time customer expectations will survive.

Supporting our urgent message above are three related guidelines:

1. The real-time organization must be agile enough to detect and respond to changing customer expectations regarding time better than competitors do.

2. The real-time organization must engage customers throughout the life of its products and services such that customers view the organization as valuing their time and, thus, meeting their needs more than competitors do.

3. The real-time organization will be transformed to value customer time through these core organizational levers: products and services, processes, data, and people.

We help current and potential organizational leaders, members, change agents, and other stakeholders interested in an organization's survival understand these guidelines more fully in subsequent chapters.

Chapter

1

The Need to Become a
Real-Time Organization

Evidence of the real-time revolution is upon us. Most customers expect companies to provide immediate service. Furthermore, they are willing to switch from those that do not. Evidence for these customer real-time pressures on companies comes from Salesforce surveys of consumers and business buyers in 2016 and 2018.[6] These surveys of over 7,000 participants in 2016 and over 6,700 in 2018 occurred in a world where almost everyone uses a smartphone. Salesforce noted, "This constantly connected lifestyle has created a culture of immediacy in which customers' definition of timely interactions means instant. *Sixty-four percent of consumers expect companies to respond and interact with them in real time.*" Salesforce also noted, "Customers expect a lot from companies, but don't have faith in them to deliver." Failure to deliver is a threat to survival, while the ability to do so provides a competitive advantage. *"Fifty-seven percent of customers have stopped buying from a company because a competitor provided a better experience."*

Even though most companies do not meet customers' real-time expectations, a number are striving to become more real-time organizations by providing faster, more convenient service. An example is Stop & Shop, a neighborhood grocer with more than four hundred stores. "We recognize that our customer is changing, and we're evolving our entire shopping experience to better serve them. They're focused on getting back to their lives, juggling many responsibilities and we want to make grocery shopping even easier and faster for them," said Stop & Shop president Mark McGowan. For example, customers can save time when shopping in-store by using a mobile app to scan items as they select them. That eliminates their waiting in a checkout line.[7]

There are many other examples of real-time customer experience transformations. Rapid ordering has been a focal point for many organizations' real-time transformations. Besides reducing the time for customers to place an order, many companies have focused on real-time transformation for their delivery of products and services, as observed through Amazon Prime and its competitors.

Customers expect organizations to provide instant responses or at least provide experiences that are better than the competition. Organizations that fail to meet these customer real-time expectations put their survival at risk. To ensure survival, leaders must transform their organizations to value customer time more effectively than competitors do.

Time: The Most Precious Customer Resource

Consider the consumer who has been in a minor traffic accident. Taking time to deal with insurance companies, getting estimates for repairs, getting repairs, and making rental car arrangements while the car is being repaired are all time drains. This unhappy consumer is already disturbed at having to spend precious time on these activities. What if the consumer encountered delays, such as being put on hold to talk with an insurance adjuster or having to wait beyond the arranged pickup time at the repair shop? Those delays would surely compound the feeling of wasting the precious resource of time.

It is not uncommon for people who are waiting on the phone or in lines at drive-up windows to drop out of the queue, aborting an intended task. Customers often consciously avoid going to establishments where lines are likely to form. As the Salesforce data indicate, customers have come to expect instant responses.

Time matters. It matters now, and it will matter more in the future when there will be continually growing demands for our individual time and attention. Time has become the most precious resource for many customers, and the value they place on it is only likely to increase. Unlike wealth, time cannot be accumulated. If a company can save its customers time, it demonstrates that it respects the high value that customers place on their precious, scarce, nonrenewable resource of time.

To illustrate how customer time could be more highly valued, consider the case of calling customer service. When a customer is told, "You are the tenth caller in the queue," this message is perceived as an improvement over the "please hold, your call is important to us" message. Being told how long it is likely to be before the customer will be able to talk with a customer service representative is even better. Customers consider more information helpful, as it allows them to better judge whether they want to invest their precious time waiting. When customers are given the option to be called back in a specific amount of time, that proves to be even better because it gives them a degree of control. They then have the choice to wait on the phone or do something else with their time while their place in line is held for them. The company that values a customer's time even more increases the number of customer service representatives to minimize any delay in responding to their customers' service needs. Immediate service from a trained, knowledgeable, and empowered source is the best real-time response to a customer's phone call. However, the company that demonstrates that it values the customer's time by designing, testing, producing, and delivering a product that needs no service reduces the need for customers to call for service in the first place. This approach is likely the ultimate winner as long as the rare service calls that inevitably will arise even under this approach are not protracted.

Chad Wright, chief technology officer at MicroAutomation and leader of the company's commercial practice, focuses on valuing customer time. "I find this missing with so many of the companies I do business with," he says. He wants his clients to recognize that time is the most precious customer resource. He advises clients who are looking at transforming via changing existing systems and processes or adopting new technologies to ask, "How will this value my customer's time?"[8] That's a powerful question!

The different examples of how companies handle customer service calls illustrate ways to value customer time more than competitors do. Companies that intentionally seek to value the customer's time have adopted the spirit of the real-time revolution. As the Salesforce research indicates, companies that are not responsive to customer real-time expectations lose customers to competitors that provide better customer experiences. The lesson here is this: Strive to become a more real-time organization. Provide better real-time customer experiences!

Real Time Is a Moving Target

The traditional meaning of "real time" is the actual time an event takes. The Salesforce research cited at the beginning of this chapter indicates that many customers expect an actual response to be an instant response.

Since most companies do not meet this expectation, customers migrate to those that provide a real-time customer experience that is closest to instantaneous.

A more recent meaning of "real time" is "immediately," which is consistent with customer expectations that companies should respond instantly. Given that most companies are unable to deliver on the expectation of an instant real-time response, companies should view an instantaneously effective interaction as an ideal real-time response. This ideal applies to interactions that customers expect to be efficient. For other kinds of experience, this ideal shifts from a minimum amount of time to the maximum quality of time spent because customers expect the experience to be enjoyable, productive, or otherwise satisfying. The ideal real-time customer experience is what real-time organizations ultimately strive to achieve. An organization becomes more real time when it provides a customer experience that is closer to the ideal than the experience provided by the competition.

Customers' expectations of the actual time it takes for a response will change as they learn what is possible via interactions with an organization and its competitors. Jeff Toister surveyed consumers over several years to learn how fast they expect businesses to respond to emails. In 2012, only 5 percent expected a real-time response of one hour or less. In 2018, the percentage with that expectation had risen to 30 percent. The vast majority, 75 percent, expected a response of one day or more in 2012. In 2018, the percentage expecting that slower response time had fallen to 56 percent.[9] These results show that "real time" is a moving target. Once customers have learned what is possible, they adjust their real-time expectations. What is possible becomes their standard for future interactions with a company and its competitors.

Customers' real-time expectations evolve as they learn over time. Customers learn based on their own experiences with their immediate provider. They also learn from that company's direct competitors. They learn from others via word of mouth or postings on the internet. Moreover, customers learn and adjust their real-time expectations based on experiences from indirect competitors. These indirect competitors do not provide products or services similar to those of the immediate provider. Nevertheless, if customers believe another company in a different industry demonstrates a greater appreciation for their time, they will expect that those techniques should be applied to a different but more immediate situation.

For example, a customer's general experience with online retailers may have led to an expectation that every organization requesting personal information should have the capability to store and display previously entered information. Rather than having to take the time to enter it again for a new interaction, it would be displayed automatically. This expectation could transcend the online retail space. For example, it could drive expectations about health-care service even if health-care providers currently fail to meet this standard. How many times have visits to a health-care provider's office required the entry of data already in the office's possession?

With more direct and indirect competitors transforming to value customer time, customers and businesses will learn that the different times associated with various steps in the life of a product or service (e.g., acquiring, using, and maintaining it) are moving targets. They will set their real-time expectations accordingly. Organizations that do not keep up with this moving target will fall behind. Given the priority that customers put on the value of their time, organizational leaders must vigilantly transform their organizations to respect that reality. Organizations that meet the moving target of rising real-time expectations will avoid the loss of customers that will inevitably befall those that fail to meet the rising bar.

A company wishing to transform a process to improve customers' time experience must first understand how customers spend their time. That includes the time to acquire and use a company's products and services. It also includes the time for any other experiences with the company, its products, and its services, such as, for example, participating in testing a product, maintaining it, and disposing of it. A business must expect that its competitors are continually upgrading their ability to improve the customer's time experience, so the goal of any rival company has to be not simply to match a competitor's time experience but to exceed it. By seeking to perform better than the competition, the successful rival company will become the industry leader in meeting real-time expectations. In this race to master time, the business that best understands how and where customers spend their time interacting with the company has the best opportunity to target its efforts to improve the customers' time experience in a meaningful way. Coincidently, this is also one clear approach to winning market share, as the Salesforce research cited at the beginning of this chapter indicates. If an organization fails to meet customers' evolving time expectations, it must provide other superior features to succeed. Those features, such as better product capabilities, quality, distribution, price, pre- and post-sale support, and ease of changing supplier, must be so attractive that they offset the less-than-optimal time experience customers will be forced to endure.

The Real-Time Continuum

Common interpretations of the term "real time" are "immediately," "here and now," "quickly," and "fast." Thus, a common interpretation of a real-time organization is that it is fast. Although a real-time organization's speed meets or beats that of competitors, that real-time response may not be demonstrating that the organization really values customer time. Being faster is important, but it is not everything that customers seek when interacting with a company. Customers ordering a Market Fresh Turkey and Swiss sandwich from an Arby's drive-through expect to be charged the correct amount, receive that sandwich correctly made, be treated with respect, and complete the transaction at least as quickly as if they had gone to a competitor. So speed is important; however, so is accuracy of the price charged, the quality of the sandwich, and the manner in which the customer is treated. If any of these other expectations are not met, the reduced effectiveness of the transaction diminishes the real-time experience.

For example, customers do not want to find that they received a different sandwich. Besides violating the expectation of receiving the sandwich they actually ordered, that would increase the time spent if they chose to have the sandwich replaced. Even if the amount of time meets or beats real-time expectations, any unmet expectations will lead customers to expect something less when they next consider Arby's. Conversely, if all goes as expected, Arby's remains a competitive alternative in the future since it would have demonstrated that it values customer time at least as well as the competition. An interaction that is fast and effective in meeting all other expectations in addition to time demonstrates that the organization values customer time.

Ideally, a real-time organization is so fast and effective that its interactions with customers are instantaneously effective. Such ideal real-time customer experiences may not be a realistic goal for all, but as more organizations strive to provide such experiences, more interactions with customers will have faster real times. Competition will raise the standard for what is considered to be fast enough. "Fast enough" is based on meeting current customer speed expectations. However, the current standard will change over time. What is considered fast enough today will be not be considered fast enough tomorrow as competition raises speed expectations.

To show progress toward the ideal instantaneous real-time interaction, leaders and organizational members striving to value customer time better than the competition can plot the real time of their customers' effective experiences on a continuum. The continuum would show the ideal and actual times the experiences take. One end would have zero, representing the ideal instantaneous real time. Assuming the real time of customer experiences is greater than zero, the other end of the continuum would have the real time that those experiences actually take. As a leader or member of an organizational transformation effort, ask questions such as, "Do we monitor the time our customers spend on product testing? Placing an order? Interacting with customer service?"

The real-time continuum can be used for several purposes. For example, it can show progress from one transformation to another. It can show progress toward the ideal real time. It can show the times for various experiences that customers view as fast enough and how those compare to your organization's times.

Organizational leaders and members can be inspired by real-time customer experiences that approach the ideal real time. For example, transferring funds from one account to another at a credit union can be accomplished almost instantaneously online. Customers do have to take time to access the account and specify the details of the transfer. Compared with pre-internet days when customers had to physically go to the credit union and have a teller make the transfer, which could have taken over an hour for those at a distance from the credit union, current real time is much faster.

For other customer experiences, real time is not so immediate. Real time could be weeks, months, or even years. Consider the time it takes to restore an antique automobile to its original condition or the time it takes to earn an undergraduate education. Thus, the real-time continuum has a range of real times, depending on the organization, product, or service and the kind of customer interaction.

Quality of Time Can Be More Important Than Speed

In some circumstances customers expect an experience that is productive, enjoyable, or otherwise satisfying. For example, utilizing a gym membership to work out or visiting the Grand Canyon is not driven by speed of the experience but instead a desire to spend time productively or enjoy the experience. Customers seeking a thirty-minute workout are not expecting the gym to provide a workout that is faster than other gyms. Rather, they expect to use equipment without waiting so that they can work various muscle groups. Visitors to the Grand Canyon are not expecting the US National Park Service to provide a faster experience than other vacation spots; rather, they expect that the awe-inspiring landscape can be experienced and enjoyed without significant impediment of crowds or delays due to parking. In these situations, the quality of time spent using the product or service is increased by the productive use of time or the pleasure experienced by these customers. The time delays and other impediments reduce the quality of the experience.

Transforming the Process of Managing Long-Term Treatment[10]

Executives at a leading North American health insurer sought to help patients manage their treatment programs for serious long-term illnesses, such as diabetes and congestive heart failure. Patients participating in an experimental health-management program received regularly scheduled calls from a team of nurses over a period of several months. The calls were designed to deliver additional support to patients undergoing long-term treatment by helping them understand the available options, sustain their treatment regimens, and reinforce lifestyle changes recommended by their doctors.

The company improved patient satisfaction with these calls not by reducing the time that the calls took but by increasing the quality of the time spent during the call. For example, the company made an effort to provide customers explicit choice on three critical elements: the type of treatment plan, the particular facility to visit, and the choice of doctors to see. In each area, the nurse was guided to tell the customer, "You have a choice; let me give you some options." Furthermore, the conclusion of the health-management calls was scripted to finish on a positive note by emphasizing the tangible insurance benefits available to patients and, where medically appropriate, the likelihood of a successful outcome to the agreed-upon action plan. These transformations of the interactions between nurses and patients illustrate that altering the process of providing long-term treatment resulted in an improved real-time experience for patients that was not measured in time but in quality of the experience.

Real-Time Management—Prioritizing the Value of Customer Time

Business leaders transform their organizations to become real-time organizations by prioritizing the value of customer time. One place to begin is to rethink what an organization can do to provide products and services faster. A comprehensive rethinking includes an examination of the time and resources it takes for various processes, such as designing products and services, testing them, and producing, delivering, and servicing them. This starting point focuses attention on improving internal efficiencies and the efficiency of suppliers. Increasing efficiency typically reduces resources, including time. Assuming increased efficiency would allow a company to provide products and services faster and at a lower cost, that could mean that the company has demonstrated that it values customer time more than previously. However, if the reduction in the organization's time does not carry over to the customer or, even worse, increases the time expenditure of the customer, the company will have failed to demonstrate that it values customer time. For example, if a company redesigns a business process to improve internal efficiencies, it may save internal time. However, if this time savings is at the expense of customer time, as would occur if the new process required customers to spend more time assembling the product instead of receiving it in an assembled state, the end result would be counterproductive. Furthermore, if the change in the company's processes made one department more efficient but forced another department to be less efficient, the change could also be counterproductive.

Consider the company that contemplated saving time by reducing product testing. Although increasing efficiency for the testing process, this change could lead to a less reliable product design, which would increase customer service time, create customer dissatisfaction, and, thus, backfire. Optimizing one process in the system of beginning-to-end processes does not necessarily lead to overall optimization.

Understanding customer use of a company's products and services is essential. Monitoring and assessing the amount of time expended, the quality of time expended, and the effectiveness of other aspects of the customer use experience would provide valuable information. Similar data collection and assessment would also be valuable for understanding internal processes and any other interactions between the customer and the organization. The resulting information would help guide transforming products, services, or processes to prioritize the value of customer time. To transform an organization to value customer time more effectively than competitors also requires similar monitoring and assessments of competitors.

Real-Time Management Research— A USC Marshall Research Project

The concepts of real-time management, the real-time revolution, and real-time organizations have been inspired by the research of Omar El Sawy and Pernille Rydén.[11] Their research found that companies that were more profitable and growing the fastest looked at efficiency and time differently than other companies. These high-growth companies considered time and efficiency from their customers' perspective. Though many companies are focused on their own time, including improving factory or logistics efficiencies, high-growth companies are focused on customer time as a journey with the company. They understand the customer journey begins upon discovering the company and continues through product or service delivery and use. More profitable companies have more ambitious time scales. They target resources to improve customers' experiences over the entirety of their journey with the company. Consider that in some cases, customers may be willing to accept a longer time period in one aspect of the journey if it allows a greater improvement in experience at other places in the journey.

Real-time management is most directly realized through fast action! It is the ability not only to make quicker decisions but also to execute the outcomes of decisions faster, sense problems and opportunities, improvise actions, take advantage of the speed of digital platforms, ingrain a rapid-response culture into the workforce, and reorganize human resources.

Real-time management puts a high priority on the value of customer time. It recognizes that the duration and quality of customer experiences are both important. To help optimize customer experiences, each interaction with customers is monitored. For example, customer interaction with a company's website can be tracked to determine how long it takes to find the desired information and place an order. Once the order is placed, other processes are used to measure the delivery of the product or service. Usage is also monitored. Support calls are tracked from the initiation of the call to the resolution of the issue; follow-up assesses customer satisfaction. Ultimately these monitoring processes are translated into value for customers via the use of that data to identify and solve customer problems. In addition, a real-time company uses the data to prioritize its transformation efforts. The business, the customer, and society in general benefit—a win-win-win situation.

For anyone, time is a precious and nonrenewable resource. If a company begins to look at time from the customer's perspective, it will begin to find ways to change products or services to save the customer time. It will also consider changing operations to recognize that the time a customer spends with the company is a resource that needs to be respected. As a result, the company will move closer to its customers. In effect, they become partners. By always striving to make customer experiences optimal, a company makes it easier for a customer to commit to working with the company. The operations that support ordering, delivering, and learning to use a product or service, as well as those that support maintaining it and disposing of it, can be complex and time consuming. Changing the product or service and time-consuming operations to recognize time as a customer's precious resource helps win customer hearts and minds. Furthermore, improving the quality of experiences throughout the life of the customer's journey with a product or service also demonstrates the company values customer time.

As leaders strive to make their organizations more real time, they will need to adapt their understanding of real-time concepts to fit their markets and operational environments. For example, leaders of Stop & Shop groceries need to understand what real time means in actual time for an average customer's total shopping time in their stores and their competitors' stores. The shorter of those two average times is one indicator of the current real time that they are trying to improve so they can make grocery shopping "faster" and get customers "back to their lives." As leaders seek to develop their views of real-time priorities that fit their unique businesses, the following points should be kept in mind:

- Since real time is determined by the customer, a company must set its clock by the customer's perception of time. An extra level of testing in the factory, which takes company time, is nevertheless likely to be beneficial if it lowers product malfunctions in the field. If a customer believes a product or service has not been usable or is faulty, the customer clock is still running. That customer requires service, which also takes the customer's time as well as the company's and opens the door for competitors with better products or better customer service.

- Real time is related to faster decision making. If the decision-making process is poor, though, the attempt to become real time can end up costing more time as a company undoes the bad decisions. Thus, faster high-quality decisions, based on solid data collected throughout the product or service lifetime, are required.

- Real time is highly dependent on the competition. A competitor with access to better data on customer real-time experiences has an advantage. If a company's transformation efforts are targeted at improving some customer time experiences, but those experiences were selected without the aid of data, they are not necessarily those most in need of improvement. The company must collect and evaluate data on customer real-time experiences to determine future improvements that are clearly necessary to meet or beat competitors.

- Product or service cost is important, but this cannot be the only driver of business strategy. For example, a customer-centric company might put a few extra nuts and bolts into self-assembly kits. The cost of the extra parts is low, and the extras save time for the buyer/assembler if a nut is lost during the assembly process. A lost nut is frustrating and takes time to recover, extending time in the customer's eye.

- For some products, customer time is driven by ordering complexity. Including in a shipment the components that allow a single product kit to take on different configurations portends that the customer does not need to decide on a specific configuration during the ordering process. A single kit can be delivered to all customers.

- For some, customer support systems are critical components in the customer's time line. Corporate decisions to provide a variety of types of support (e.g., technology-supported, service-oriented chat rooms, email, chat boxes, and efficient call-in numbers) are appreciated by customers in environments where different customer segments may have different support expectations and needs.

- Achieving product, service, operational, or technology changes that recognize customer time as a critical resource will likely require more than a few employees to recognize the value of customer time. Consider whether the situation also requires time and resources for changes in strategy and culture that will fully support responding with other needed changes.

Joining the Real-Time Revolution

A real-time organization values customer time. Its leaders adopt a customer-centric view of the importance of time. They continually work with employees and other stakeholders to transform the organization to value customer time more effectively than competitors do. This continual striving to value customer time means the organization has joined the real-time revolution.

Helping customers save time is a tangible demonstration that the company has the best interests of the customer at heart. Besides helping customers save time, companies engaged in real-time management strive to ensure that expenditure of customer time satisfies customers' expectations of high-quality experiences. High-quality experiences (rather than fast, effective experiences that save time) are particularly relevant when customers expect their interactions to be enjoyable, productive, or otherwise satisfying. When a company accepts that customer time is precious, it has the opportunity to win the hearts and minds of customers. It has the opportunity to compete successfully. It has the opportunity to survive and thrive.

Organizations that have not joined the real-time revolution have leaders who have not adopted a customer-centric view of the importance of time. These organizations are more likely to provide challenging customer experiences, view customers less admirably, and face a dimmer future. When websites are difficult to navigate, when ordering and status verification are complicated, when assembly instructions are difficult to follow, and when obtaining customer support is burdensome, these difficulties demonstrate that the company considers the customer insignificant and unimportant. As a result, customers will seek out competitors who provide better customer experiences. The migration of customers away from organizations that are not focused on valuing customer time threatens their survival.

Companies, regardless of how good they are today, must continually drive themselves to improve the duration and quality of time associated with customer experiences. The constantly connected lifestyle with its culture of immediacy has driven customers to expect instant responses from companies. Customers do not hesitate to switch companies for better experiences. This customer behavior is cause for companies to reconsider the way they interact with customers and assess success. Rather than assessing success primarily by traditional measures that are inwardly focused, companies would be wise to accept that the duration and quality of time customers expend interacting with them, their products, and their services also serve as valid measures of success.

For example, the real time of customer interactions should be measured and managed intentionally throughout the life of a product or service, from beginning to end. Examples of stages in that life include design, testing, production, delivery, use, maintenance, and disposition. Customer interactions must be actively managed, not as independent programs for each life stage, but as an orchestrated whole. This change in perspective is an essential element in driving the real-time revolution. It changes how real-time organizations measure their relationship with their customers. Leaders who are seeking to transform their organizations to become real-time organizations are the revolutionaries who are defining the future of business.

Key Takeaways

- The real-time revolution is upon us. As an organizational leader, join the revolution by helping your organization transform to value customer time better than competitors do. Organizational survival is at stake. The big risk is losing customers to organizations that also join the revolution.

- Time has become the most precious resource for many customers. The value they place on it is only increasing.

- Real time is the actual time an event takes. It is a moving target. Customer expectations of the time it actually takes for a specific interaction with an organization, its products, or its services will change as the customer learns what is possible.

- A common interpretation of a real-time organization is that it is fast. Ideally, a real-time organization is so fast and effective that its interactions with customers are instantaneously effective. In reality, though, not all customer experiences are so immediate. Real time ranges from instantaneous to weeks, months, or even years. Thus, real time is a continuum of effective real-time customer experiences. Instantaneous experiences are at one end. Longer experiences are placed toward the other end.

- Real-time leaders put a high priority on the value of customer time. They recognize that the duration and quality of customer experiences are both important. Fast, effective experiences that save time are important when customers expect the experience to take little of their time. High-quality experiences are important when customers expect their interactions to be enjoyable, productive, or otherwise satisfying.

- Understanding customer interactions with your company, its products, and its services is essential. To develop that understanding, start by asking questions similar to these: "How do we monitor the time our customers spend on product testing? Placing an order? Using our product? Interacting with customer service? And how do we similarly monitor competitors?"

Real-time organizations do not simply minimize the time customers must spend; instead, they optimize customer experiences to meet expectations. That allows them to retain customers, survive, and thrive. Customer expectations are determined by customer experiences. In this constantly connected world with its culture of immediacy, customers demand a new level of obsession. Companies must customize customer experiences from the start to the finish of the customer journey. Based on understanding customer expectations, companies must understand when to design relatively fast, effective experiences as well as when to judiciously design experiences of high-quality engagement.

Chapter

2

The Real-Time Monitoring and Response (RTMR) System

Companies that utilize Internet of Things (IoT) technologies to actively monitor equipment installed at their customer sites have the opportunity to respond to problems more quickly to reduce downtime. Repairing products that are out of service more quickly than competitors demonstrates greater respect for the value of customer time. Advances in technology have made it increasingly feasible to add features to almost any product to make it both smart and connected to the internet, thereby allowing usage and diagnostic data to be collected throughout the product's life. In many cases these smart products can even be repaired by remote technicians.

For example, consider the blood- and urine-analysis equipment made by Sysmex ($2.5 billion in sales on the Forbes Global 2000 list for 2018 [12]). Sysmex originally added connectivity to its instruments to "perform quality control on customers' instruments, monitor their operating status in real time and support their stable operation." In doing so, Sysmex reduced the amount of time to service equipment because the equipment could self-report detailed diagnostic information, which allowed service calls to be scheduled before the customer knew there was an issue; furthermore, the monitoring data always provided the service technician enough information about the problem to enable appropriate preparation to solve the issue. Service technicians can now access as much information about a machine when they are off site as when they are on site. Often they can fix the problematic device by remotely rebooting it, delivering a software upgrade, or talking an on-site medical technician through the repair process. As a result, Sysmex's service costs, equipment downtime, and customer satisfaction improved dramatically, making it more competitive.[13] Companies such as

Sysmex that are better at reducing disruptive equipment downtime are more real time than their competitors.

Becoming a real-time organization means that an organization has established and regularly employs a real-time monitoring and response (RTMR) system. Organizations employ these systems to do three things:

- Collect time-centric and other data, such as sales, costs, performance of competitors, environmental issues, and government regulations. This data is collected by monitoring a variety of activities and conditions internal and external to the organization.

- Analyze the data to identify strengths, weaknesses, threats, and opportunities and prioritize the areas to improve; for example, financial statements and strategic analyses are commonly generated and used for these purposes.

- Respond to changing conditions reflected in the analyses by specifying the requirements for change that will lead to improvements, developing or acquiring innovations that will meet the specified requirements, and implementing those innovations.

A real-time organization's RTMR system builds on the existing monitoring and response system. Importantly, it adds an overarching focus on valuing customer time. That focus assures that the system includes data that supports the evaluation of the organization's competitive strengths and weaknesses in valuing customer time. It also assures that the organization responds to competitive challenges that threaten its successful delivery of better customer real-time experiences. The RTMR system is an essential element for determining the transformations required to compete effectively as the real-time bar is raised by the competition.

It also allows an organization to draw a picture of its real-time status compared to competitors (see Figure 2.1). The organization's chances of retaining existing customers and attracting new ones (i.e., surviving and thriving) increase as it moves toward becoming a real-time contender or leader. The likelihood of customers migrating to its competitors increases as it moves in the other direction toward real-time denial.

For products and services that are based on remote intelligence, technologies such as IoT can be used to collect and monitor product status and usage statistics. IoT data, when collected and centrally analyzed, can be employed to identify faults and supply detailed diagnostic information to the manufacturer. Advanced RTMR systems can often

Figure 2.1 Continuum of Real-Time Organizations

detect systemic faults before the customer has realized there is a problem. The same data can also be utilized to monitor usage statistics that provide the basis for predictive fault management, allowing the manufacturer to respond before a fault has occurred. Finally, the same data, when combined with data from other customers, can provide more generalized quality statistics that often allow a manufacturer to segment between user-derived faults and more wide-scale product design issues. For companies that deploy products and services based on intelligent devices, those devices facilitate building an RTMR system that moves the company toward becoming a real-time contender or leader.

An effective RTMR system supports three foundational activities for a real-time organization:

1. **Monitoring Customer Real-Time Experiences.** To remain competitive, a real-time organization should collect data to determine how well its products are saving customer time or providing greater value for the time spent. Such data ideally provides verifiable proof that a company's efforts yield incremental customer value above and beyond competitive offerings. The same data can be employed to indicate additional areas where the company might provide new features or services that bring additional value to the customer, e.g., by saving incremental time.

2. **Prioritizing Areas for Improvement through Understanding Competitive Positioning.** A detailed understanding of where and how a customer interacts with a company's products may provide a basis for comparison with a company's competitors as well. Developing an understanding of where the organization stands relative to competitors can clarify current areas of strength and weakness in efforts to demonstrate value for customer time. The clarity of strengths and weaknesses provides the foundational data for prioritizing areas for further real-time transformation targets.

3. **Specifying the Response to the Market.** RTMR data can also be used to drive a variety of innovations, including offensive and defensive innovations. The successful real-time organization has an RTMR system that provides a detailed understanding of the customer's product use that can be applied to specify the company's innovative response to the competition (e.g., new product innovations, new marketing campaigns, new complementary services, etc.). Those individuals in a real-time organization's RTMR system who are responsible for specifying the required outcomes of an innovative response will be driven by the goal of transforming the organization so that it values customer time better than competitors do.

Foundational Activity: Monitoring Customer Real-Time Experiences

Companies must collect data to monitor the amount and quality of time customers spend using their product or service. As just one example, consider fast-food restaurants. For each sales transaction restaurants can store a variety of data, including an identifier for the specific transaction, its location and date, the time the order was entered, the time the order was completed, and the items ordered. In addition, restaurants can use online surveys to ask a number of questions about the customer's experience. To assess the customer's quality of time spent, questions may ask for ratings of satisfaction with several items, including the speed of service, the accuracy of the order delivered, and the taste and quality of the food. The online survey data can be linked with the data previously stored for a specific sales transaction through a matching survey code that the customer enters from the transaction receipt. Upon completing the survey, the customer may be given a validation code to redeem an incentive for completing the survey, e.g., a free sandwich or dessert at their next visit.

Besides asking current customers who are driven by expectations of efficient interaction, as in the fast-food example, consider a range of other customer types, conditions, and monitoring approaches. First-time versus repeat, infrequent versus frequent, high versus low volume, current versus potential, and current versus those who are no longer patrons are examples of different types of customers. Examples of different conditions include interactions driven by customer expectations of efficiency versus expectations that the time spent will be enjoyable, productive, or otherwise satisfying; other examples include high versus low price and rarely versus frequently purchased products or services. Different approaches to monitoring could include using hypothetical ("what if") versus actual scenarios; also, consider using observational studies of customers in addition to asking them or as an alternative approach to monitoring. Indeed, consider monitoring with various combinations of customer types, conditions, and approaches.

Leaders of real-time organizations will also want to know the answer to this important question: "Do we value customer time more than our competitors do?" Real-time organizations must collect data not only to monitor the amount and quality of time customers spend using their products or service, but they also must collect similar data on the competition. If a company's customers are also customers of the competition, these customers can legitimately answer how the company rates against the competition. Data collection that asks a customer to compare one establishment with competitive establishments provides valuable data that can be used to assess how well the company and competitors stack up against each other.

Ideally, data collection should be automatic and unobtrusive, i.e., not requiring the customer to spend any time providing information (e.g., to enter data or answer questions). As an example, consider the use of smart wearables. An Apple Watch can automatically monitor and report on the owner's activity.[14] Though some customers may consider this an invasion of their personal privacy, others are willing to provide activity data to companies they support and trust in an effort to help make their favorite products and companies even better. As a further example, consider the futuristic scenario where a consumer has a wardrobe full of smart clothes, i.e., clothes with embedded sensors that report usage statistics to the clothing producers, clothing wear data to the dry cleaner or tailor, and gift ideas to family and friends. Based on a customer's personal preferences and patterns of use obtained from monitoring, the technology could even help a consumer select a daily outfit and recommend matching items of clothing for future purchase.[15] This kind of unobtrusive monitoring could simplify the customer's life by allowing simpler maintenance of the wardrobe, speeding up the dressing process, extending the life of the clothes, and making it easier to expand the wardrobe.

If data collection requires customers to enter data or answer questions, a company could offer incentives or thank-you gifts in exchange for participation in a favored shopper program. The number of participating users could increase dramatically, particularly if such rewards were interpreted as further evidence that the company values the time required for customer participation. However, companies should be cautious. If they share the data with other companies, those receiving companies must overtly demonstrate their appreciation of the customer's time or they could negate the goodwill initially created through the program. Further, each receiving company has indirectly agreed to honor the original company's data policy. However, the original company will suffer the customer's wrath if the receiving company violates the customer's trust.

Besides collecting data by monitoring product or service use, a real-time company will also want to collect data on other customer experiences associated with the product or service. Examples of such data include the results of participating in product design or testing, behavioral data associated with the product or service ordering process, performance data associated with product delivery, and records of product maintenance activities. As the company evolves toward a real-time company, it will want to build and maintain a map that details various customer interactions. These customer interactivity maps should include time and experience quality metrics, which provide quantitative and qualitative indices to evaluate current and future performance.

The design of the data collection part of the RTMR system involves a number of choices. The data collected should support developing an understanding of customer expectations, experiences, and values. The ultimate goal of that understanding is to transform your organization to value customer time better than competitors do. Questions to consider include:

- Which customer experiences do we want to monitor?
- What methods do we want to use to collect data on the duration and quality of customer experiences?

- Do we want to monitor all customers? If not, how do we want to select customers to monitor?

The importance of customer expectations regarding time and other factors affecting their behavior suggests additional questions, including:

- How do we want to collect customer data on expected duration and expected quality of their experiences?

- How do we want to collect data on the value of reducing time or increasing experience quality?

- How do we want to measure the trade-offs customers are willing to make among time and other factors?

Similar questions about competitors should also be asked. Although comparing customer experiences across companies may not be straightforward, the design of the RTMR system should provide the foundation for evaluating real-time progress in customer experiences.

With the emergence of sensor-detected data and the Internet of Things, the alternatives for collecting data have begun to expand significantly; these evolving systems provide a wide range of new metric possibilities. As an example, consider the situation where a company wishes to improve its understanding of how customers operationally use its products. The company might initially design a product to automatically detect and provide detailed diagnostic information to the customer support desk. To further expand the value of this information, the same data could be copied and sent to the product development team so that it can use that incremental knowledge to improve product enhancements already in progress. Going further, the same data could also be provided to the product management team to aid its efforts to create a new usage-sensitive pricing model. And finally, the same data could be routed to the marketing team so it could design messaging and marketing campaigns that highlight the most useful features of the product. Such monitored data could provide regular, consistent, and detailed feedback that would be valued by everyone in the organization concerned with ensuring an optimal customer experience.

The goal is to be able to determine the amount and quality of time each customer spends in each stage of an ongoing engagement. Ultimately, the data on customers' experience can be leveraged to drive a management-level dashboard. A company may find it helpful to think about customers as resources that dynamically flow through different processes related to a product or service. The overall goal, as a real-time company, is to accelerate the rate at which customers flow through these processes or improve the quality of customers' experiences as they flow through one or more of these processes. Monitoring customer real-time experiences is an essential foundation for determining where and how to demonstrate that the company values customer time more than the competition.

Ideally, the monitoring system should go beyond collecting data on customer interactions during the marketing and sales process, use of the company's products and services, and experiences with various support personnel. Similar data must be collected on potential customer interactions with the competition for benchmarking purposes. This data horizon should be extended to monitor indirect competitors that influence customer expectations. Competitive customer experience data will be more challenging to collect and will not provide as detailed an understanding as proprietary data; this is to be expected, but by monitoring competitors' activities, their efforts to improve their processes will be detected and can, thus, be acted upon.

For example, in the education field, university faculty, staff, and administrators are responsible for designing educational programs for traditional four-year undergraduates. Staff should also monitor direct competitors (i.e., comparable universities with similar four-year undergraduate degrees) and indirectly competing institutions (i.e., competitors that offer educational alternatives). Examples of such alternative educational options include community colleges offering two-year degrees, universities offering three-year degrees, and providers of online courses, as well as corporate training programs designed to provide nondegree educational opportunities for their employees.[16]

Ultimately, an RTMR system should collect data on the amount and quality of time customers spend with the company—integrating data from marketing, sales, product and service usage, and customer support functions. Overall, it should track customers' real-time experience at various touchpoints with the organization and its competitors. The goal is to allow a company to understand what the bar is for demonstrating that it values customer time more than direct and indirect competitors.

The real-time revolution makes it imperative that a company actively collect and analyze such monitoring data. That tracking information is essential for the organization to respond appropriately and move toward becoming or maintaining its status as a real-time contender or leader. Without such monitoring data, the organization may be in real-time denial, in danger of losing its customers to those using a data-based approach.

Foundational Activity: Prioritizing Areas for Improvement through Understanding Competitive Positioning

Monitoring customer real-time experiences (the first foundational activity of the RTMR system) is essential, but it is not sufficient for becoming an effective real-time organization. The company needs to use that data to help it prioritize opportunities for improvement. Assuming a company has established a real-time monitoring system, it will have the ability to evaluate its performance compared to the competition, just as the customer would measure the company's competitive effectiveness. Given that companies are motivated to differentiate their products, services, and customer experiences from each other, it is likely that a competitive comparison will highlight strengths and weaknesses between competitors. With such data, a company could choose to improve performance in an area where the competition outperforms it, or it could target improvements to an alternate area, e.g., it could focus on further extending an area of strength.

Prioritizing areas for real-time improvements can be approached in several ways. For example, a company could start by examining strengths and weaknesses in customer real-time experiences. To obtain different perspectives on what those strengths and weaknesses are and how they should be prioritized, a company could analyze data from a sufficiently varied set of customers. To illustrate, customers could be segmented into those who expect a high-quality experience in researching a product and those who expect to conduct little or no research. Differences and similarities between these segments could then be examined.

As another example of an approach to prioritizing, consider that the customer experience may span multiple activities. A set of evaluators could assemble the data so the end-to-end experience can be understood in its entirety. As a leader, consider asking, "Do we want to develop this understanding with just our own people?" Alternatively, supplement internal resources with independent evaluators, or opt to outsource the process completely. For example, evaluators could include not only members of the organization but also supply chain partners, immediate customers, and, potentially, competitors' customers.

To illustrate an end-to-end analysis, assume that a point of disparity emerges from the data that demonstrates customers take longer to make use of the company's product than a competitor's product. Perhaps the same data also indicate that the company has a more effective product support process compared to the same competitor. Based on its understanding of the data, the company could choose to highlight the importance of customer support in its marketing efforts and use the available data to demonstrate superior performance in this area. Presumably, this same data could be used to initiate a new transformation program intended to improve the time to operate the product with the caveat that operational improvement proposals should not undermine the product support process. The priority would be to drive real-time product improvement in a way that avoids driving real-time inefficiencies in other areas of the customer interaction process.

Developing a list of priorities from the analysis of the evaluators is essential for identifying the areas for improving customer real-time experiences. Understandably, all companies are resource constrained. Once a prioritized view of opportunities has been identified, companies must be selective in choosing which areas will be targeted for improvement programs. The opportunities that cannot be covered with available resources become candidates for successive rounds of transformational improvements, with the understanding that each successfully completed program should be considered a baseline for future improvements.

Prioritizing Areas for Improvement—The RSI Example[17]

Republic Services Inc. (RSI) is the second largest service provider for domestic nonhazardous solid waste disposal in the United States. The company's customer service demands are incredibly intensive insofar as RSI provides continuous on-the-ground services for thousands of communities across the US. These customers produce over 12,000,000 calls per year. To complicate matters, customer needs are distributed across 50 call types and 150 different call reasons. To support these highly complex customer service requests, RSI employs approximately 1,200 service representatives in over 100 locations.

With such a large-scale and complex operation, providing seamless customer service posed a significant challenge. Agents sometimes lost or dropped customers' phone calls, or customers hung up in frustration. What is more, when RSI call centers became busy, agents and supervisors lacked current data about the call center, such as which agents were available. Without this information, agents could not adapt effectively to changing call volumes, resulting in customers experiencing increased wait times.

Customers exiting a call queue were required to furnish information they had already entered. Furthermore, RSI agents often needed to confer with other agents to resolve issues. However, agents encountered difficulty conferring with one another in a timely fashion. Because agents did not know whether certain agents were available, it became necessary for them to try different numbers to locate an agent who could assist or take a transfer. The delays created by these bottlenecks often led to impatient customers hanging up or being dropped as they were transferred to agents who were busy or simply not available to assist.

In evaluating the most significant problems, RSI identified the following areas for improvement as the highest priorities:

- Decrease number of dropped calls and customer hang-ups

- Decrease agent response time

- Improve inter-agent communication

- Provide agents with operation-critical call center information

In addition to possessing monitoring data about real-time customer experiences to identify highest priority problems, RSI's evaluators must understand the context of the customer experiences to interpret monitoring data on those experiences. For example, evaluators could look at the data from monitoring that shows customer wait times, dropped calls, and agent response time and identify those as problem areas without knowing anything about the call center context; however, if they were given a narrative description of the call center context in conjunction with the monitoring data, it is more likely that evaluators would identify inter-agent communication and lack of operation-critical call center information as high-priority problem areas that need to be addressed to help improve agent response time, dropped calls, and customer hang-ups. The inclusion of the last bulleted priority suggests that the evaluators were given such a narrative.

RSI's efforts to reduce problems with dropped calls, customer hang-ups, and customer wait times clearly are related to how well an organization values customer time. However, as presented, the RSI case study is silent on how the company compares with direct or indirect competitors in these areas. For a company to become or maintain its status as a real-time contender or leader (see Figure 2.1), it is essential to compare how well the organization performs against its competitors. As more organizations join the real-time revolution, increased competitive emphasis will be placed on solving customer-focused time concerns. Those organizations that do not move toward competitively better real-time operations are in danger of falling behind.

Foundational Activity: Specifying the Response to the Market

The third part of an RTMR system is specifying the intended results of the prioritized responses (based on the second part of the RTMR) from evaluating the monitoring data (from the first part of the RTMR system). Armed with an improved understanding of how customers spend time with it, the company will take action to improve real-time experiences for its customers. The intent of changing the experiences is to demonstrate that the company values customer time better than competitors do. To guide implementation of changes, the intended results of the changes must be specified. Changed experiences occur when the company implements innovations based on these specifications.

To illustrate the specifications of an innovation, consider the RSI case presented above. In this situation, RSI customers recognize that service problems may occur. Such problems drive a need for customers to interact with RSI agents. The overall intended result for RSI and the customer is to reduce the total time a customer spends with agents to resolve the problem completely.

The following is an example of the specifications of an innovation to reduce aggregate customer resolution time (and the more detailed intended results that make the overall result possible):

- Agents must be able to view information about customers quickly so they can converse about their issues from a source of customer-specific knowledge. The necessary information should be provided to agents within three seconds.

- Agents (and customers) should not spend undue amounts of time with process inefficiency. The solution must eliminate the need for customers or agents to enter information more than once. Information must flow between agents seamlessly.

- Agents should be able to know which other agents are available, their areas of specialization, and customer interaction histories so the problem can be quickly referred to another agent as needed. Some problems will require escalation to a problem specialist.

RSI Next Step[18]

RSI adopted a software application that allowed agents to access information they required about their customers without being forced to toggle between different windows or applications. All the information agents needed was at their fingertips immediately. The solution also empowered agents to create a more personal interaction with customers by greeting them by name and by being apprised of their past issues, as well as those they were calling about. As one agent noted, "Customers really appreciate not having to wait a minute or two for the agent to pull up their record." Agents were also able to see which other agents were available to collaborate on certain customer issues.

Specifying an innovation can be viewed as similar to specifying software requirements. Similar to software, the innovation could be developed internally or externally, or it could be acquired from a provider that already has a fully developed solution. The specifications (i.e., requirements) of the innovation provide a basis for guiding development or for evaluating solutions from external providers.

Going beyond the Foundational Activities: Responding by Innovating

The innovation process begins with the understanding that change needs to occur and then goes beyond to design the innovation so that it becomes realizable. Finally, the innovation must be made tangible. Innovative efforts must be incorporated into a company's regular operations so they can bring to life the company's desire to demonstrate that it tangibly values customer time. Implementing such real-time innovations into a company's regular operations is no easy task. Given the importance and challenges associated with innovation, much has been written on it.[19]

It is likely that a corporation's culture will be changed by repeated cycles of (a) monitoring how well customer time is valued, (b) determining the innovations needed to respond to shortfalls or opportunities for doing better than competitors at valuing customer time, and (c) incorporating those innovations into regular operations. To deal with cultural change issues, a cohesive focus on a common objective is essential. For companies joining the real-time revolution, that means focusing and orchestrating their efforts around serving the customer's understanding of the value of time.

Transforming Your Organization and the RTMR System

Leaders, in conjunction with organizational members, must transform their organizations to value customer time more effectively than competitors do. This can only be accomplished by continually transforming the organization through innovations that recognize the changing nature of customer real-time expectations. An RTMR system is an essential enabler of such transformation; it is the ultimate determinant of progress. The RTMR system includes the foundational activities—monitoring customer real-time experiences, prioritizing areas for real-time improvements, and specifying innovations to better value customer time—that lead to transformational programs. Furthermore, the RTMR system generates and implements the innovations, i.e., the transformational programs that subsequently are measured by their ability to provide change that is valued by the customer.

Transforming an organization is not a one-time event—it is an ongoing revolution. Leaders of real-time organizations, in concert with their members and other stakeholders, regularly sense and respond to changing customer real-time experiences; in addition, they also strive to transform the RTMR system to sense and respond to changing customer expectations more rapidly than competitors do. The RTMR system provides the basis, the North Star, which empowers leaders to guide their organizations forward through competitive and uncertain terrain.

Key Takeaways

- A real-time organization's RTMR system adds an overarching focus on valuing customer time to the organization's existing monitoring and response system. This overarching focus guides organizational leaders and members to evaluate their competitive strengths and weaknesses in valuing customer time. It also directs them to continually strive to improve customer real-time experiences.

- An organization's RTMR system tracks customer real-time experiences when they interact with the organization, its products, and its services. It also tracks the real-time experiences of competitors' customers.

- Organizations that are real-time leaders, real-time contenders, and real-time transitionals use data from their RTMR systems to help them identify real-time strengths, weaknesses, threats, and opportunities relative to their competitors. Data analysis helps them answer the question, "What customer interactions with us, our products, and our services are our highest priorities for improving customer real-time experiences?"

- The highest priorities for improvement guide the specification of the results that innovations should achieve to respond to needed improvements. Innovations that meet these specifications must be implemented to improve customer real-time experiences.

- The specifications for innovations provide the basis for guiding either the development of innovations or the evaluation of innovations already developed by external providers. Once developed or acquired, these innovations must be incorporated into the company's regular operations. Leaders of real-time organizations, in concert with their members and other stakeholders, make these organizational changes possible. These transformations provide the improved customer experiences that demonstrate that the organization values customer time better than competitors do.

- The big picture for organizational leaders is this: If you have not done so already, join the real-time revolution. Engage in an ongoing process of monitoring and responding to changing customer real-time experiences. Furthermore, recognize that the RTMR system is a work in progress. Improve it as well. The resulting transformations should reinforce your organization's survival as well as its progress toward thriving as a real-time contender or a real-time leader.

3

Levers for Becoming More Real Time—A Product/Service Life-Path Perspective

Dell rose from a dorm-room start-up to a global force during the 1990s as a PC maker. Michael Dell launched Dell Computer Corporation in 1984 with $1,000 and a few employees. By 1995, the company grew to more than seven thousand employees in fifteen countries with $3.5 billion in sales implementing a build-to-order direct sales model. This success validated Michael Dell's belief that tailoring personal computers to user preferences would make Dell computers easier to use and troubleshoot. The company became known for its relatively affordable but high-quality PCs, reliable customer service, and strong customer relations. Although some other companies also offered build-to-order PCs at low prices, they were not considered comparable to Dell's quality. Dell offered a large product variety specified by the customer with short assembly and delivery lead times. That was accompanied by reputable customer support and attractive prices. As a result, Dell competed effectively with much larger competitors in the personal computer market, including IBM, Apple, and Compaq.

These competing companies offered product lines that gave the consumer little product variety, had lead times of weeks or months due to backlogged orders, and were generally more expensive than the newer Dell platforms. Dell's success was built on a mass customization strategy, incorporating the use of modular components, clever use of web-based configuration-to-order, efficient assembly, and just-in-time inventory management. This strategy allowed Dell to compete on high volumes, low cost, and speedy delivery and still offer a quality product with reasonable variety and reputable customer support.[20]

Dell made innovations in the following areas:

- **Product Design.** Dell designed modular components that could be configured at the time of ordering into a customized product to meet individualized customer needs.

- **Product Orders.** Dell designed a web-based interface where customers specified the configuration of modules that would meet their individual needs.

- **Production and Delivery.** Products were built and delivered quickly to individual customer order specifications using efficient assembly, logistics, and just-in-time inventory management.

- **Product Use.** Dell PCs were seen as high-quality, low-price PCs, designed to meet specific user preferences, and easy to use.

- **Service.** Customer service was reliable. Support could be matched to the customer's ordered PC, making it easier to troubleshoot problems.

In this example, a real-time effect occurs at each stage where Dell made innovations. In several of those stages, the amount of time the customer spent waiting on that stage was reduced. For example, the time to design a product to individual preferences was reduced because of the innovative modular product design; the time to service the product was reduced because the service representative knew what to expect from each computer. In some stages the real-time effect increased the quality of the time for customers. For example, the ordering process helped customers discover their specific computer needs.

Together, these stage-specific real-time experiences contributed to the customer's overall real-time experience. Based on the positive effects across the various touchpoints, Dell customers maintained a more positive real-time experience when compared to the competition.

What may not be obvious is that a company can also affect stage-specific and overall real-time experiences through its activities that do not involve direct interactions between the customer and the product or company. In Dell's case, the company's innovation in product design that led to the modular components may not have involved direct interaction with the customer. Nevertheless, the results of Dell's innovative product design activity could then be used by the customer to specify a customized PC. Dell's innovative product design activity is an example of an indirect activity that contributes to real-time experiences by making it possible to reduce the amount of time or increase the quality of time spent in subsequent direct interactions between the customer and the company or product.

The stage-specific and overall real-time effects occurred not because of independent attempts to innovate at each stage but because of a coordinated effort to follow an overall business strategy across multiple stages of customer interaction. That strategy recognized the importance of meeting customer preferences on several criteria, including rapidly providing a customized, high-quality product at low cost. Dell experienced phenomenal growth from 1984 to 1995, going from a start-up to a $3.5 billion company.

A portion of Dell's success can be attributed to its ability to tangibly demonstrate that it valued customer time better than competitors did. Leaders in a company aspiring to emulate Dell's success will be facing a different set of competitors as they look to innovate in a way that best provides value for its customers. An obvious question for leaders to ask is, "Where should we look to innovate?"

Where to Look to Innovate:
A Product/Service Life-Path Perspective

Monitoring customer real-time experiences involves mapping their interactions to the company's organizational processes and collecting data on those interactions. Such a map serves to identify strengths and weaknesses, thereby providing a valuable tool to prioritize areas for potential real-time improvement. Potential areas for improvement must first be mapped to specific innovations that promise to realize the needed improvements. The goal of any proposed real-time improvement should be to demonstrate that the organization values customer time more effectively than competitors do. The measure of the innovation's success (or lack of success) would be captured by the RTMR system. That measure should reflect the change in how the customer spends their valued time.

It is essential that the company adopt a methodical approach as it seeks to understand the time investment customers make when they choose to interact with the company. The approach adopted here focuses on the steps in the life of a product or service (see Figure 3.1). These steps include customer touchpoints as well as processes that do not directly touch customers but have an effect on their real-time experiences. These steps occur along the life path of a product or service, beginning with the initial steps in creating a product or service. They continue through the steps that produce the product or provide the service. Furthermore, they extend to steps in the ongoing use of a product or service as well as steps that go beyond that until its end of life.

Many organizational leaders will find that the steps in the life of a product or service provide a suitable framework to understand and measure customer interactions. For others, a different framework may be more suitable (for example, one that is more sales/marketing focused). Whichever framework is selected, it is imperative that the structure provide a rigorous and structured means to uncover potential areas where innovative changes might be made to demonstrate that the organization values customer time more effectively than its competitors.

Figure 3.1 illustrates multiple touchpoints where customers interact with the company and its product or service. The most obvious touchpoints occur during usage, but some companies may choose to involve customers beginning at product inception and continuing throughout the life of the product or service. When investigating places to innovate, an organization should consider improvements to any process that changes a customer's real-time experiences. Small improvements to processes that are frequently experienced can provide significant value improvements for the customer. Similarly, modest improvements at a time when

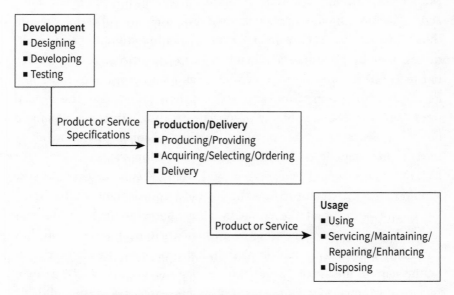

Figure 3.1 Steps in the Life of a Product or Service

customers consider their time value heightened can also create positive valuation improvements.

The examples below illustrate innovations along the life path of a product or service. The examples start with innovations occurring at the bottom right of Figure 3.1 and move up and to the left. Some examples illustrate innovations that occur at a step that directly involves interaction with customers. Others indirectly affect customer real-time experiences.

Usage Innovation: Nudie Jeans[21]

A customer typically determines what happens to a product at the end of its life. A simple disposal process that requires a minimum of time can be considered a positive demonstration of real-time value. Some retailers and manufacturers have developed programs for their customers to recycle or rejuvenate their products at the end of the perceived product life. These programs extend the life of products that retain some residual value.

For example, the Swedish denim company Nudie Jeans offers free denim repair. Instead of discarding their old worn-out denim, customers may bring them in to be renewed. In 2017, 49,235 pairs of jeans were repaired worldwide. Extending the life of a pair of jeans contributes to sustainability. That is not only good for the environment but allows the customer to obtain more value from the product. In addition to offering free denim repair, Nudie Jeans also offers customers who are ready to dispose of their jeans a 20 percent discount on a new pair of jeans if they trade in the old pair. Trade-ins are repaired and then sold in Repair Shops all around the world. This procedure had been operating for two years when, in April 2018, Nudie Jeans began offering an online repair kit.

When buying clothes, customers are balancing a number of decision criteria, e.g., clothes quality, price, and, in this case, the environmental effects of recycling and the time to recycle. Nudie's repair program reinforces the company's commitment to quality. It tangibly backs that commitment by ensuring that customers have the means to extend the life of their clothes. It also provides an environmentally friendly means of disposing of the jeans at their end of life. Nudie Jeans' two years of success with their repair and reuse transactions via their Repair Shops, followed by their online expansion, demonstrates that customers responded favorably to the company's efforts. Nudie Jeans provides them with a favorable balance of time, environmental values, and economic values compared to other competitors.

Product and Usage Innovation: Apple

Cell phones have become an essential part of the way people live their lives. Apple understood that when a phone is running low on power, customers want to charge it fast. Time becomes a critical resource. Apple innovated with the iPhone 8, 8 Plus, and X to charge noticeably faster than previous iPhones. In doing so, it demonstrated its appreciation for a customer's perception of time. With the correct cable and adapter, customers can recharge these iPhones' batteries up to 50 percent in thirty minutes.[22]

Product and Usage Innovation: Dyson

Before leaving home for the day, people often groom themselves. When rushing to make a scheduled appointment, time can become a critical concern. Dyson created an innovative hair dryer that has been engineered to protect hair from extreme heat damage, with fast drying and controlled styling.[23] When asked to evaluate Dyson's hair dryer, one customer reported, "I've been using Dyson's Supersonic hair dryer for a year, and I swear by it . . . Heat damage can promote split ends and even hair loss, but Dyson's smart heat control system measures air temperature 20 times a second, so you're never exposed to too much heat. I have thick hair, but it only takes me 10 minutes to get it completely dry with this dryer—it's a major time-saver in the morning."[24] The Dyson hair dryer demonstrates a respect for customer time by allowing for rapid grooming while at the same time reducing the risk associated with a rushed grooming process; a rushed process can cause damage that needs to be repaired, resulting in a missed appointment. Alternatively, it could cause a bad impression, undermining the quality of the appointment time.

Service and Usage Innovation: Bullet Trains[25]

Low-cost travel options have created a culture where travel is a way of life. People do not stay in one location but travel between locations with increased frequency, with the time spent in transit often being considered unproductive time. The Shanghai Transrapid bullet train runs the nearly nineteen miles from Shanghai's Pudong International Airport to the Longyang Road metro station on the outskirts of Shanghai. It takes just over seven minutes at 267 mph to complete the journey using magnetic levitation (maglev) technology. Japan is celebrating the fifty-fourth anniversary of high-speed train travel. In 1964, the Hikari high-speed train launched service between Tokyo and Osaka, cutting travel time from nearly seven hours to four by rail. Japan's H5 and E5 series Shinkansen provide a network of high-speed bullet trains that connect destinations at 224 mph. Italy's dueling train operators, NTV and Trenitalia, each boast a high-speed train that connects Milan to Rome in about three hours at speeds of 220 mph. These train operators understand that customers want to minimize the time they spend in transit; furthermore, they also understand that efforts to make the time productive and comfortable increase the quality of the necessary customer time investment.

Clothing manufacturers, smartphone providers, hair dryer producers, train manufacturers and operators, and many other organizations are innovating to make their products and services faster. That demonstrates that they value customer time more effectively than their competitors do. The innovations noted here, like many others, not only address speed but other criteria as well, including increasing sustainability, reducing product downtime, reducing risk during use, and improving experience quality. These additional criteria reinforce the recognition that both the amount of time customers spend using a product or service and the quality of that time investment are important. Improvements to both can be leveraged to demonstrate an organization's respect for customer time.

Figure 3.1 also serves to illustrate that companies can demonstrate customer value by process innovations that involve production and delivery of a product or service. These places to innovate may or may not include a touchpoint where the company and customer directly interact.

Included in the steps of producing a product or a service are the processes that involve interactions between the company and its suppliers. Although these processes may be untouched by customers, they remain areas where a company may want to innovate. That is particularly the case when these processes affect the company's ability to compete more effectively on the quantity or quality of time experienced by customers in later steps in the life of a product or service.

Production Innovation: OSRAM and Bosch[26]

Most manufacturers build products utilizing production equipment where the output from one manufacturing device feeds another device throughout the production floor. OSRAM, based in Munich, is a global lighting manufacturer with many such production devices. OSRAM worked with Bosch, which has expertise in connectivity, to develop a production innovation called the OSRAM Ticket Manager (OTM) with a number of requirements, including these:

- A smart central system to replace personal handling of individual machines
- A process that assesses and documents the condition of all machines
- A way to assign maintenance and repair tasks

Connecting over eighty different machines at OSRAM's Berlin location, OTM supports employees by taking streams of data from different production devices and processing them into useful information. Workers now simply consult a mobile app for a status report on the factory's machines. Maintenance tasks can be efficiently scheduled, and a clear overview of any upcoming tasks can be planned and coordinated.

OSRAM looked at its production process as an innovation opportunity. The company understood that it could achieve traditional goals of increasing productivity and quality by managing the factory as a system rather than managing each individual machine separately. Although OSRAM's innovation does not include any direct touchpoints for the customer, the automation program allowed the factory to become more agile, thereby allowing OSRAM to be more responsive to changing customer needs.

Furthermore, increases in quality mean customers spend less time seeking support after a purchase. Organizations that intentionally focus on understanding customer real-time experiences across all the steps in the life of a product or service are more likely to identify and implement the most impactful innovations. This benefit can only be realized if the innovation evaluation process considers the larger context, which includes both processes with and without direct customer touchpoints.

Production Innovation: Datex

Online shopping is a growing part of retailing. The customer need not spend time traveling to a physical store but can browse through an online catalog and place the order in a virtual shopping cart. This real-time experience saves the customer time by eliminating the need to visit brick-and-mortar competitors. Websites that minimize the time (and frustration) that it takes to find a desired product and complete a retail order prove their real-time credentials by understanding the precious nature of a customer's time. Amazon Prime, for example, has spurred a lot of innovation and disruption as Amazon seeks to deliver products in real time. Amazon's efforts to demonstrate value for the customer's time have increased expectations and made performance targets for supply chain companies a moving target.

Datex is an independent supplier of logistics management software. It understands that supply chain delivery times and complex risk management programs require end-to-end logistics visibility to achieve meaningful results. "We're noticing a huge push and pressure on the fulfillment side to get orders turned around on a much faster scale and pace than a lot of the technology is capable of doing today," says Michael Armanious, vice president of sales and marketing at Datex. "What normally would have taken less than an hour, all of [a] sudden needs to go out within minutes."[27]

These two examples show that faster is better, but it is speed in support of the customer's understanding of quality that matters. For example, at OSRAM it is speed in the production process while still assuring product quality. At Datex, it is speed in the delivery process while still managing associated risks, such as assuring that the right product is delivered undamaged. The real-time experience of a customer who is served quickly but without accuracy or respect might achieve an improved immediate response time. However, forcing the customer to endure a less-than-satisfying interaction or invest additional time to address the inaccuracy undermines the speed. A customer might be delighted to learn that an order has been filled quickly, but the relationship with the company can quickly sour once the customer discovers the order has not been properly filled. Leaders must strive to ensure that a company's innovations lead to customers perceiving that the organization values their time more effectively than the competition.

Figure 3.1 also illustrates that real-time innovations can take place during the product or service development process. The development process includes the product/service design, development, and testing processes. Depending on the development philosophy adopted by a company, these steps (and any associated sub-steps) could include direct customer touchpoints that impact the real-time nature of the company, or these steps may be more indirect real-time processes. Indirect real-time process improvements are not immediately visible to the customer, but they have a customer-visible impact via steps later in the life of a product or service. Thus, these processes are potential places to make innovative changes that demonstrate a company's respect for the value of their customers' time. Decisions made here will have significant effects on subsequent steps that directly affect customer real-time experiences.

Development Innovation: Tripping.com[28]

Although customers want "perfect" software, they are often willing to accept minor issues provided the discovered errors are promptly addressed. Tripping.com provides a vacation and short-term rental service and makes use of an iterative, participatory approach to testing its website. Colin Gardiner, VP of products and analytics, stated, "Don't wait, get testing! Time is the most valuable resource we have and when you're not testing, you're not getting results that take time to get." By approaching website development as one large test, Tripping.com is able to quickly capture customer experimental data, develop hypotheses that drive continuous improvements, and prioritize testing processes. Its goal is to provide visitors with a fast and intuitive search of its wide range of accommodations around the world. And by incorporating users into a controlled testing process, it is constantly discovering new ways that it can improve the customer's experience. The objective is to increase agility to evolve their service faster than the competition, thereby contributing to making the company more real time. Through such a constant testing process, Tripping.com is better able to anticipate customer needs and offer information that aids customers in creating their dream vacations.

Implications for the RTMR System

The RTMR system provides a map of the customer's real-time experiences over the life of a company's products and services. It should also provide a comparable map for the competition. These customer experiences will change over time as customers, the organization, and competitors evolve. As a result, the data in the RTMR system has to be maintained through an active monitoring system.

The customer experiences monitored in the RTMR system should be mapped to a company's processes, thereby allowing the company to focus real-time improvement efforts on processes that drive maximal time benefit to the customer. Figure 3.1 illustrates a simplified set of processes in the life of a product or service that can be mapped and monitored in the RTMR system. An organization could choose to monitor more processes than those that involve customer interaction. Also monitoring processes that do not involve customer interaction should yield a more complete picture than monitoring just processes that involve customer interaction. As improvements are made to any monitored process, analysis of the RTMR system data will highlight the effectiveness of those efforts. Simultaneously, the RTMR system will highlight changing customer behaviors that could signal the need for a reprioritization of a company's continuing improvement efforts. Analyzing a more complete set of processes will generate a richer analysis and interpretation of current status, problems, and opportunities required to demonstrate that a company values its customers' time better than the competition.

In addition to innovating with products and services, various customer touchpoints, and other steps along the life paths of products and services, organizational leaders must consider the RTMR system itself as another major place to innovate. The RTMR system becomes a company's innovation heart monitor. It measures performance against the competition and makes it possible to sense and respond to changing customer real-time expectations. Over time, the monitored information coming from customers will increase. Understanding of customer behavior will also increase. Steadily enhancing the data monitored by the RTMR system will increase the visibility of opportunities and challenges organizations face as they continually seek to improve their real-time performance.

Levers for Innovation

An organization's appreciation for customers' perceived investment of time comes from analysis of the data that the RTMR system collects. This analysis provides a data-driven definition of real time based on customer experiences. It permits the organization to explore innovation opportunities that can be selectively pursued as the organization seeks to increase the real-time value it provides its customers. Innovation opportunities can be found at each of the steps in the life of a product or service.

The most important levers for redefining and optimizing the manner in which a company competes in the marketplace will vary by company. Nevertheless, the potential core levers for specifying innovations at each step in the life of a product or service include the following:

- **Products or services.** Example: A product's operational features could be enhanced to increase its operational speed. Such an innovation program could begin by upgrading the product components provided by partners and suppliers.

- **Processes.** Example: The processes for entering an order could be refined to make them faster and to include additional checks to reduce order errors. Such an innovation program could check product inventories for order fulfillment purposes. When inventories fall below acceptable levels, the revised process could automatically notify partners and suppliers.

- **Data.** Example: Analytic processes could be initiated when established objectives are not being met. Such an innovation program could be triggered when targeted delivery times are missed. That could lead to the understanding that the factory is unable to maintain suitable inventory levels. That realization could lead to the identification of a specific machine that requires increased maintenance.

- **People.** Example: A company decides to empower employees to open trouble tickets on behalf of customers. This empowerment provides incremental incentives for employees who act to solve problems before customers need to invest incremental time to resolve open issues. To implement this innovation, the company chooses to train employees in basic customer support techniques so that they view themselves as part of a support team that ensures that customer interactions are fast, error-free, and respectful.

Each of these core levers is described more fully in its own chapter to follow. Levers beyond the core levers are also described in a separate chapter. These additional levers include the product or service technology, culture, strategy, and relationships with suppliers, partners, and customers in the organization's ecosystem.

Based on analysis of the data that a company collects via its RTMR system, organizational leaders and members of the RTMR system will identify a set of potential levers for changing customers' real-time experiences. Use of a framework, such as the steps in the life of a product or service, guides the collection and analysis of data by the RTMR system. It helps assure that the total impact of a product or service on the customer's perception of time, including both amount and quality, is considered. It also provides confidence that appropriate areas for innovation have been considered from beginning to end of the life of a product or service. This beginning-to-end perspective contributes to prioritizing alternative innovation programs.

Transforming an organization into a more effective real-time organization that will survive and thrive requires prioritizing and addressing prospective innovation programs based on available resources. Leaders understand that to compete effectively in the real-time revolution, improvement programs must be structured and managed to provide the largest customer benefits. Using the levers for innovation to transform the organization must demonstrate that the company values customer time more effectively than competitors do.

Key Takeaways

- As an organizational leader, consider how to answer this important question: "To value customer time more effectively than the competition, where should we look to innovate?" The approach adopted here to help answer this question focuses on looking at the steps in the life of a product or service.

- ▸ These steps begin with the initial steps in creating a product or service, such as designing, developing, and testing a product or service.

- ▸ They continue through the steps that produce the product or provide the service, which also include ordering and delivering the product or service.

- ▸ Furthermore, they extend to steps in the ongoing use of a product or service as well as steps that go beyond that, such as maintaining and disposing of a product or service at its end of life.

- All of these steps involve processes that are potential places to make innovative changes that demonstrate a company's respect for the value of customers' time. Changes in processes earlier in the life of a product or service will affect later processes. Together, innovations at various steps in the life of a product or service affect customer real-time experiences.

- The RTMR system should monitor customer experiences that occur at various steps in the life of an organization's products and services. It would also be informative to monitor processes that do not involve direct customer interaction. Monitoring and analyzing a more complete set of processes will generate a richer analysis and interpretation of current status, problems, and opportunities required to demonstrate that a company values its customers' time better than the competition.

- Innovation opportunities can be found at each of the steps in the life of a product or service. The most important levers for innovation at each of these steps will vary by company. Potential core levers at each step, though, include products and services, processes, data, and people. In addition, leaders can consider using levers beyond the core levers to improve the value of customer time. These additional levers include changes to the product or service technology, culture, strategy, and relationships with various stakeholders. The core levers and those beyond the core are the subject of the next chapters. Singly or in concert, these levers provide the innovations that transform your organization into a more effective real-time organization.

4

Using the Product or Service Lever to Transform to a More Real-Time Organization

TaskRabbit realized that many people are always pressed for time. Its success is evidence that many people do not want to spend their scarce time to complete necessary chores. By building a network that lets users hire independently contracted "taskers" to perform chores, TaskRabbit helps people maintain their busy lifestyles. Since being acquired by furniture retailing giant IKEA in 2017, the company has been expanding rapidly. There's an obvious synergy between the two businesses: consumers can buy furniture at IKEA, then hire someone from TaskRabbit to assemble it. With TaskRabbit's integration into the IKEA.com site, customers can check the availability of taskers based on location and product choice and start the process of booking a tasker while shopping online. Customers can buy IKEA furniture and have it assembled as soon as the next day.

According to Stacy Brown-Philpot, CEO of TaskRabbit, the easy availability of help to assemble IKEA products has boosted online sales. She notes that "we've seen more customers now will buy things online through the IKEA website—and buy more things—because the TaskRabbit service is available." Indeed, one recent IKEA customer set a TaskRabbit record, hiring helpers for 117 hours of furniture assembly.[29]

The convenience of scheduling this furniture assembly service while completing a purchase makes the scheduling faster for most customers. For many customers, hiring someone to assemble the furniture has proven to be an attractive substitution for do-it-your-self assembly. Customers choosing this option spend none of their scarce time on assembly, making the effective real time for that option zero. Assuming the assembly is done properly, that is a real-time customer experience that demonstrates respect for the value of customer time and makes IKEA products more attractive to purchase. Although the actual real time for assembly is not instantaneous, it can occur as soon as the next day. IKEA has clearly used the service lever to become a more real-time organization. Although currently unable to offer same-day assembly, innovating to offer that is obviously a path to becoming even more real time.

Pulling the "Faster" Real-Time Product or Service Lever

The product or service is the overt reason the customer interacts with the organization—products and services fill needs. However, in a competitive market, customers have choices; there are almost always alternative ways to fill a need, and in those situations the customer employs selection criteria to decide between different alternatives. Increasingly, the primary selection criteria for a product or service include customers' time expectations. Research indicates that convenience makes it possible to decrease time and effort in acquiring and using a service. It also indicates that convenience is at the forefront when customers evaluate their service experiences.[30] Customers will gravitate to the product or service option that reduces the amount of time they spend on a nonpleasurable activity. Modifying a product or service to allow customers to complete a nonpleasurable activity faster is an important transformation lever to consider. It is important, though, to understand the bounds of the task. For example, if customers are making airline reservations, they expect that the reservations will be completed quickly; however, they will not consider the task of making reservations finished unless and until the reservations have been made completely and correctly.

Innovation with Boarding Passes[31]

Boarding passes were once issued by hand at the airport check-in desk. Inventory and seat allocation were handled manually, being either handwritten or accomplished using stickers to ensure that once passengers had a seat it would not be given to someone else.

Migration to electronic ticketing was completed in 2008. By 2010, 2D bar-coded boarding passes replaced the previous generation of more expensive magnetic stripe boarding passes. That meant passengers could check in online and print their boarding passes at home. Because magnetic strips required expensive Automated Ticket and Boarding Pass printers and were printed using a special type of expensive paper, this transition to home check-in provided a significant cost saving for the airlines and an added convenience for the customer. Home computing was booming, and boarding passes were easily printed on demand employing a simple home printer. Changing from the magnetic strip to bar-coded boarding passes took many years and millions of dollars of investment. But this investment was offset against the enormous savings made by the airlines with reduced airport check-in costs and reduced passenger processing costs. Projections at the time of the transition were that the industry would save up to $1.5 billion every year.

However, accepting passenger-printed boarding passes introduced new security risks that required additional attention, given intensified security requirements. Ultimately, it was determined that a new approach was needed to verify boarding pass authenticity within the airport. The machine-readable component of a bar-coded boarding pass contains the details for the flight, including passenger name, date of travel, airline, flight number, origin airport, destination airport, and class of travel. The format also allows for extra information to be appended to the bar-code data stream, enabling airlines to adapt their business processes to add additional services such as frequent flyer or trusted traveler programs. Because the machine-readable information is standard, it can be read and understood not just by the issuing airline but by third-party scanners and applications at key points in the passengers' journey, for example, at government-managed security checkpoints. Today, airport security is managed through a mix of airport-printed passes, passenger-printed passes, and mobile passes. Passengers who check in early via online access and print their own passes not only reduce airline and airport costs, they save themselves time and stress while giving the airport more time to validate their identity.

Growing consumer adoption of smartphones and tablets, coupled with declining sales of home printers, means that this successful home check-in model has continued to evolve. The next generation of mobile boarding technology could be based on NFC (near-field communications), which utilizes wireless communications from mobile smartphones so customers are not required to present a paper boarding pass or QR code or pass a bar code through a scanner; they would simply stroll on board and the technology would flag their presence.

Airlines and airports have successfully been able to reduce the costs associated with managing boarding passes while simultaneously reducing the time it takes a passenger to obtain a boarding pass. By making it easier for customers to acquire boarding passes and by enabling the boarding pass technology to speed them through the airport check-in process, the transportation industry is moving its markets toward the real-time world.

Changing the boarding pass process required the participation of not just a single airline but multiple members of the air transportation industry. That included those responsible for security to assure adequacy and authenticity of the boarding pass. Given the role the boarding pass plays in air travel and the number of coordinated participants in the air travel network, the innovation required an industry-level agreement. Part of that agreement included the specification of the carrier-specific data fields that allow the airlines to add airline-specific information to the standardized check-in information. These proprietary data fields allow the future possibility for a specific airline to gain a real-time competitive advantage over other airlines based on proprietary service options.

In this example, no single airline was the beneficiary of an immediate competitive advantage. The whole industry benefitted from cooperation among competitors and other key stakeholders. Faster customer service was made possible by the transformation of processes. Those transformations were enabled by technology changes. Faster service came along with the changes that were driven by lower costs. All airlines gained a service and cost foundation from which individual airlines could provide future improvements to customer real-time experiences.

So, what is the lesson from this example for leaders aspiring to transform their organizations to real-time organizations? The lesson will become clearer after considering the following example from Fandango.

Innovation at Fandango[32]

Fandango touts itself as the go-to destination for more than thirty-six million moviegoers each month. Fandango helps movie fans discover new films, buy tickets, and share their passion for movies. It entertains, informs, and guides film fans with trailers and movie clips, exclusive and original content, insider news, and expert commentary. As the company claims, "We make it easy to find and buy the right movie at the right time, with showtimes and ticketing to more than 26,000 screens nationwide. Fandango is available online, and through our award-winning mobile and connected television apps with over 46 million downloads and counting."

According to the company, "Mobile Ticket is the latest, fastest way to get tickets from Fandango." Once you complete your purchase through the Fandango app or website, you receive a digital ticket on your mobile phone that allows you to skip the line at the theater box office.

Fandango clearly recognizes that moviegoers do not want to spend time waiting in line to buy tickets at the movie theater. Moreover, Fandango recognizes that moviegoers want them to provide a fast purchase experience. Fandango responded with Mobile Ticket as its latest ticket-purchasing innovation.

Innovation with tickets at Fandango was not as complex as innovation with boarding passes within the airline industry. Unlike the airlines, which had to collaborate with competitors and other stakeholders, Fandango did not need to collaborate with competitors. Furthermore, competitive benefits for individual airlines were not the reason for boarding pass innovation.

As the question posed earlier basically asked, how, then, is the history of innovation with boarding passes instructive for leaders of real-time organizations? Consider this lesson: To provide customers with better real-time experiences, think innovatively across the entire ecosystem. Think innovatively about those you need to work with to become a more real-time organization. Think innovatively about the results you intend to obtain. Think innovatively about what needs to be transformed to achieve those results. Think innovatively about what levers will enable the transformation. Take advantage of other transformations. Build on good business practices, such as lowering costs. And think innovatively beyond the immediate transformation to what your next innovations could be.

The expectation is that as complexity and interdependence increase, companies will increasingly work with external stakeholders to more completely satisfy customer desires. The implication is that activities of a company's broader community can be supportive of the drive to become a real-time company, or they can undermine those same efforts. From a customer's perspective, there may be no obvious line of delineation between a company and its partners. A real-time company that works with slower or more poorly performing partners will fail to meet customers' expectations. Increasingly, companies will discover that to achieve the next level of performance along the real-time performance continuum, they must work with their partners to improve their real-time performance.

The transformations by Fandango and the airline industry involved process changes that were enabled by technology. Technology can make dramatic improvements possible, such as the dramatic cost reductions experienced by the airline industry. One of the most dramatic changes in customer real-time experience occurred with Netflix.

Innovation at Netflix[33]

In 1998, Netflix launched the first DVD rental and sales site, netflix.com. In 1999, Netflix debuted a subscription service, offering unlimited DVD rentals for one low monthly price. Netflix mailed movies to customers, who then returned them. It could take days for customers to get the movies, and it took time and effort to return them. In 2007, Netflix introduced streaming, which allowed members to instantly watch television shows and movies on their personal computers. From 2010 to 2016, Netflix launched its service in various countries so that it is now available worldwide. Members can instantly watch TV series, documentaries, and feature films across a wide variety of genres and languages anytime, anywhere, on any internet-connected screen.

Using enabling technology to reengineer its processes, Netflix disrupted its industry. Through transforming its service from delivering physical DVDs to streaming entertainment over the internet, Netflix has become a quintessential real-time organization. Rather than having to wait days for entertainment to arrive through the mail, customers can receive it instantaneously upon request. This achievement shows that leaders can transform their organizations to provide ideal real-time customer experiences.

Pulling the "Better Quality" Real-Time Product or Service Lever

The primary value of a product or service from the customer's perspective of time may be to provide the customer with a more satisfying (e.g., enjoyable or productive) use of time. If that is so, then changing the product or service to provide the customer with a more satisfying use of time is an important transformation lever to consider. However, the quest for time quality does not give the real-time company a license to violate customer time duration expectations. Based on prior experience, customers have developed a set of time norms that shape their views about how much time an activity should take. For example, when consumers go to the movies, they certainly expect the time that it takes to get their tickets and popcorn to be short. In addition, if they expect a two-hour feature-length film, they are not going to be satisfied with a fifteen-minute short film even if the quality of the short film exceeded every expectation.

The history of the movie theater experience makes for an informative case study that demonstrates how theater owners have continuously sought new and innovative ways to improve the entertainment experience for their customers. In effect, by improving the quality of the time for the theater audiences, they increased the time value for their customers.

Innovation with the Movie Theater Experience[34]

Vitascope Hall opened its doors to the general public in New Orleans in 1896. At the time, theaters provided a mix of live performances supplemented with short films and newsreels; no other theater in the US had ever been designed with the sole purpose of displaying motion pictures. Since then, movie theaters have evolved tremendously with the incorporation of concession snacks, plush seating, sound-shaking technology, and 3D visuals.

In 1925, Paramount installed the first air conditioners in a movie theater in an effort to improve customer comfort and improve the quality of the time customers invested to see a film. In 1925, popcorn was also introduced into cinemas when Charles Manley developed the first electric popcorn machine. He specifically targeted movie theater owners when marketing his product because people became hungry when watching a film, and popcorn increased their enjoyment of the event without disturbing the other patrons. With the 1930s came the introduction of candy into concession stands. As these snacks increased in popularity, the concession stand became a more and more prominent and expected addition to the architecture of each theater.

From the beginning, numerous experimental attempts were made within the theater itself to merge audio and visual entertainment. When *The Jazz Singer* first spoke to audiences in 1927, the talking picture revolution took hold as patrons responded to this more complete entertainment experience. Since the emergence of the "talkies" in movie theaters, audio configurations have never stopped evolving. From the original monaural audio feed, the cinema industry moved toward a stereophonic configuration to provide an audible sense of movement within the auditorium. The arrival of surround-sound technologies in the 1980s allowed sound mixing engineers to further enhance the feeling of movement by allowing the source of the sound to change from the screen at the front of the theater to the rear of the auditorium. Continued refinements in sound technology have allowed sound engineers to enable flyover effects, seat-shaking bass sounds, and many other environmental effects (e.g., a spaceship hovering and moving above the audience). The goal of these immersive sound systems is to more completely engage the audience by creating a sound environment that transports the moviegoer into the heart of the action from each seat in the theater.

For cinema exhibitors, immersive sound was perceived to be one of the best ways to differentiate themselves from home entertainment with large flat-screen TVs. However, home entertainment has not stood idly by. It, too, has continued to evolve the quality of in-home entertainment systems. These consumer-grade systems are now capable of bringing a high-quality surround-sound theater experience to the home, thereby forcing theater owners to seek other methods to differentiate their services. Many theaters have taken steps to improve the quality of their seating, some have reconfigured the theater to resemble a restaurant where food and drinks can be served, and many employ reserved seating options to allow the patrons to select a specific seat for a specific show.

During the 1980s and '90s, almost every movie was produced on 35mm film; it was the standard for movie production and distribution to theaters. As a physical medium, film was difficult to work with; the production process was a slow and manual operation. Once the film was complete, copies had to be physically duplicated and distributed to theaters. At the end of the twentieth century, the University of Southern California, working with the entertainment industry's Digital Cinema Initiatives (Disney, 20th Century Fox, Paramount, Sony Pictures Entertainment, Universal, Warner Bros., and others), created a new digital standard to support the film industry. This new standard allowed digital technology, first developed for the computer industry, to be reapplied to the film production process. Not only did this new technology improve production processes, it also allowed for the incorporation of computer-generated special effects and editing into the workflow. Further, by moving the film distribution system from a process that physically shipped 35mm films (via overnight shipping) to individual theaters to a distribution process where content is electronically delivered to the theaters over a digital network, other benefits are achieved.

Manual shipment of films is a slow, labor-intensive, and expensive process. By moving to a digital distribution system, there are significant operational cost savings, and theater owners can easily alter their presentation lineup. For example, if a multiplex theater owner discovers one film is in high demand, it is a straightforward process to configure the theater so that particular film is showing on multiple screens. By allowing local theater owners greater flexibility to cater to local film interests, the potential for sold-out showings is reduced and customer satisfaction is increased. It also expands the theater owners' options because they are now able to do more than show films at their theaters. They can also support corporate events and broadcast live events happening anywhere in the world. Because customers can more easily see their desired film or event, the quality of the time they spend at the theater is further maximized. In the year 2000, there were just thirty movie theaters in the world set up with digital screens. A decade later, there are more than thirty-six thousand.

As screen sizes got larger, the resolution of the content became more important. High-resolution content has a sharper image and can be shown on a large screen without degradation of the image quality. The resolution of a movie shown in a digital cinema is measured by the horizontal pixel count, so 2,048 $\times$ 1,080 pixels for 2K or 4,096 $\times$ 2,160 pixels for 4K. Ultimately, the quality of the movie that a customer will see in a theater will depend on a number of factors, such as the screen size and available lighting, but the resolution of the content is the limiting factor around which the other parameters are set. As the entertainment industry continues to press to further improve the content quality for its customers, an increasing number of production and display systems are being developed to increase the value that customers derive from the time they have invested to watch a film.

It may be that future innovations in the movie theater experience will further improve picture and sound quality, seating options, food choices, or other aspects of entertainment. Immersive experiences based on new technologies like augmented reality (AR) and virtual reality (VR) may emerge to support personalized content enhancers or more completely immersive experiences.

The industry understands that (1) consumers want to be entertained, and (2) there are a growing number of options for the consumer to choose from. Consumers will seek to maximize the entertainment value of their time when deciding between the various options available to them.

Innovation in a competitive industry is a nonstop process; companies must innovate to survive. This is especially important in hypercompetitive industries where there are significant direct and indirect competitors. In the entertainment industry, a consumer has many options so companies, like theater owners, must compete not only against other theater owners but also against home entertainment services, live events, nightclubs, and even the board game industry. When services are dissimilar, customers will weigh the cost and time investment for their options, paying clear attention to perceived differences in the expected value of their time spent, including both quality and duration.

The goal of most innovation or transformation efforts is to improve quality, reduce costs, or create new or better opportunities. Most companies will measure the success of such innovations based on their ability to improve an internally defined metric. Theater owners' move toward the adoption of digital technology was motivated by a desire to reduce costs. Happily, this same transformation also made it easier for them to manage the content they showed and be more responsive to changing customer desires. From a real-time perspective, any innovation should improve the customer's real-time experience and drive other business values for the company (such as lowering cost). However, improving the customer's real-time experience is not always the driver of innovation, particularly for organizations that have not joined the real-time revolution. For example, if the entertainment industry had moved away from overnight film shipping before there was a digital alternative, that would have lowered shipping costs, but the shipping process would have taken longer, and that would have negatively impacted the industry's ability to support theater owners and, ultimately, the moviegoing customer.

When properly applied, innovations that improve the customer's real-time experience have a compounding effect. In the case of the digitization of the entertainment industry, application of digital technology to the production process has improved production efficiencies. That time saving can be used to get movies to market quicker, or the extra time can be reinvested to improve the film quality (via more special effects, more editing, etc.). This same technology, when applied to the distribution process, provides additional process improvements that benefit the customer. However, when one well-meaning process innovation (e.g., reducing the cost of overnight shipping without a digital alternative) causes another process to slow, the intended benefit can be completely negated.

Innovation with iRobot[35]

iRobot was founded in 1990 by Massachusetts Institute of Technology roboticists with the vision of making practical robots a reality. In 2002, iRobot launched the first Roomba vacuuming robot. There have been a number of innovations since then. A review of the Roomba 980 by a user in 2015 notes that the 980 is her third Roomba. She finds that these robots have cut down on cleaning considerably. Before Roomba, she vacuumed every day. The Roomba keeps her house tidy; however, since she recognizes that Roombas do not vacuum as well as a regular vacuum, she vacuums really well once a week or sometimes every other week. While the Roomba is keeping her house clean on a daily basis, she works on something else, and then the house is clean enough for her to enjoy. She muses, "It is good to have a robot maid to help you keep the daily stuff tidy."

A later Roomba model, the Roomba i7+ with Clean Base Automatic Dirt Disposal, holds thirty bins of dirt, dust, and hair. A 2018 review notes, "Robot vacuums get smarter with each generation, and iRobot's Roomba i7+ might just be the most advanced model we've tested to date. In addition to Amazon Alexa and Google Assistant voice control, multistory mapping, and adaptive camera-based navigation that cleans better as it learns your home's layout, it's the only vacuum we've tested that can empty its own dustbin. Sure, it's a little loud, and at $949.99 it's one of the most expensive models we've seen, but it's also the only robot vacuum out there that doesn't require you to lift a finger. And isn't that why you want one in the first place? For its truly autonomous cleaning capabilities, the Roomba i7+ earns our Editors' Choice for high-end robot vacuums."

iRobot itself states, "With more than 25 years of leadership in the robot industry, iRobot remains committed to building robots that provide people with smarter ways to clean and accomplish more in their daily lives."

When customers use iRobot Roomba vacuums, they spend less of their scarce time vacuuming than they would with a regular vacuum. They still need to pick up shoes, toys, and other clutter before turning loose a Roomba, but they can use the time that they would have used vacuuming to do other things, i.e., be more productive ("accomplish more in their daily lives"). iRobot is becoming a more real-time organization by striving to achieve an ideal combination of customer productivity and satisfaction with the experience of using a Roomba. It is using the product

innovation lever to provide customers with real-time experiences
that meet and raise their quality-of-time-spent expectations.

Concluding Thoughts on Innovating
with the Product or Service

It is essential for a company to understand how its product or service
impacts customers' time experiences. Customers critically evaluate
their experiences when using a specific product or service. It is important to recognize that they also look beyond those usage experiences
to consider a more holistic view of time; they will consider every step
associated with a product or service as being part of their time investment with that company. Efforts to transform the way customers use
a product or service are important, but the company must also look
beyond that horizon to consider the other steps that customers take to
discover, acquire, and support the company's products and services. For
example, if a company alters the design of a product (such as an automobile headlight) so that it is quick and easy for customers to replace
while maintaining the usable life of the product, this redesign demonstrates that the organization understands and values the time customers
invest not only in using the product but also in replacing it.

When a company begins a program to transform itself into a more
real-time company, it has to expect that its competitors are undergoing their own real-time transformations. As competitors move toward
becoming more real time, the organization's survival will become dependent on its ability to continuously improve its real-time performance. For
the company to be sufficiently agile in such an environment, it must continue to monitor and respond effectively to competitor-driven changes to
customers' time expectations.

As illustrated with the examples in this chapter, a company may opt
to modify or enhance its product or service to make the product faster
or the service more engaging. Such an enhancement may be the optimal
course of action for demonstrating that the company values customer
time more effectively than competitors do. However, using the product
or service lever to counter competitive threats is not the only lever available to a real-time organization. For example, improving its ordering,
delivery, or support processes could be considered. In such a competitive

situation, the goal for the responding company is to use the levers at its disposal to transform customer expectations in its favor.

Key Takeaways

- When searching for a product or service that is to be used to perform a nonpleasurable activity, such as vacuuming, customers will buy something that they expect will conserve their scarce resource of time. They will want to reduce the amount of time they spend on the activity. Transforming a product or service to allow customers to spend less time on such an activity or complete it faster is an important transformation lever to consider. It is also important that the activity be done completely and correctly.

- When searching for a product or service to provide a satisfying use of time, customers will buy a product or service that they expect will be enjoyable, productive, or otherwise satisfying. Changing such a product or service to provide the customer with a more satisfying use of time is an important transformation lever to consider. It is also important to take related customer time duration expectations into account.

- Some transformations are fairly straightforward. Some are not. As a leader aspiring to transform your organization to a real-time organization, think innovatively. Think innovatively about those you need to work with, the results you intend to obtain, what needs to be transformed, and the levers that will enable the transformation. Take advantage of other transformations. Build on good business practices. And, like a good chess player, think ahead. Think innovatively beyond the immediate transformation to what your next innovations could be.

- Innovation in a competitive industry is a nonstop process. Companies must innovate to survive. Innovations or transformations other than real-time transformations generally seek to improve good business practice, such as increasing quality, reducing costs, or creating new or better opportunities. As a leader, consider pursuing real-time transformations that will improve both customer real-time experiences and good business practice. Leaders in real-time denial run the risk of threatening survival if they pursue transformations that would improve business practice while at the same time worsen

customer real-time experiences. This unhappy threat is particularly likely when competitors provide better customer real-time
experiences.

- Efforts to transform the way customers use a product or service are
  important. However, leaders must also look beyond use and consider
  the other steps in the life of a product or service. Those include steps
  where customers discover, acquire, and maintain the company's
  products and services. Furthermore, using the product or service
  lever to counter competitive threats is not the only lever available to
  a real-time organization. The following chapters discuss a number of
  levers. In responding to a competitive situation, one or more levers
  may be used to transform customer experiences so customers view
  their experiences more favorably.

Chapter

5

Using the Process Lever to Transform to a More Real-Time Organization

The smartphone is a handheld personal computer and communications system. Smartphones have provided an explosive vehicle for real-time organizations to digitally transform processes. Numerous retail stores such as Home Depot and Walmart have launched applications that allow their customers to place orders from home or from their mobile devices and then pick up the purchases at the store while they are running day-to-day errands. Stores provide special designated parking areas and special counters so customers can readily walk in and quickly pick up their purchases.

Moreover, when a brick-and-mortar store gives customers the ability to browse online before visiting the store for the purchase, it is allowing them to make better use of their time. The fact that a store has a physical presence also provides the shopper with the ability to see a product of interest before purchasing. Having both options permits customers to choose a browsing experience that may be independent from the purchasing process. By offering both options, customers can decide on their approach to browsing. Not all browsing strategies are the same for all people or applicable for all products.

Consciously or unconsciously, customers move from first deciding they have a product need, then to acquisition and use, and finally to product retirement. Customers go through a series of identifiable processes that move them through that journey. Each process represents a series of activities that customers, employees, suppliers, and other partners must complete to move through the life of a product or service. Some processes require interactions between participants, whereas others build on the outputs from the prior steps. One example of a process is the development of a new product or service. Another example is producing a product. Still another is the customer's use of the product. Within each process are a series of detailed steps that must be achieved to complete the overall process. Each of these steps in every process represents a potential core lever to be optimized in an effort to transform an organization to become more real time.

A real-time organization understands that time is a critical component of the customer experience and that any effort to change the steps in a specific process should result in an improved real-time customer experience. For example, if the steps required to deliver a product to the customer could be changed so that delivery time is reduced from a week to two days or even less, these changes have the potential to improve the customer's real-time experience. If the customer recognizes that the new delivery time is better than the competition, this transformation will stand out as tangible proof that the organization understands the value of the customer's time better than its competitors.

Process-related levers for transformation include the procedures, physical resources, and personnel used for each step. The physical resources include materials that become part of the product or service, supplies that are employed during the process, and tools that support the process. In the digital age, the tools that are utilized in the process ordinarily include digital interfaces, which produce data; accept data entered by employees, customers, or others; and display results. The tools also include an information and communication technology (ICT) system connected to the interface. The ICT system accepts data from the interface and may transmit it, combine it with other data from other processes, manipulate it, and return results. For example, a factory-based machine can support an interface to a system that manages the entire factory line, and it can also feed data to a spreadsheet-like display on a dashboard that allows management to monitor the process for deviations in production. As a lever for transformation, the dashboard can be changed to automatically highlight significant deviations in performance and automatically shut down the line if critical operational parameters are exceeded.

Before deciding that using the process lever is a priority, the company must understand how proposed changes improve both product quality and the real-time perception of the company by its customers. If the company decides the net improvement to the customer experience justifies pursuit of such a transformation, it must first analyze the people, tools, data, data flow, and ICT system support required to make such a transformation. The necessary changes would then be identified and implemented by the company's staff, its suppliers, and its partners as appropriate.

More effectively valuing customer time should be the overarching driver of all processes selected for transformational activities through analysis of data in the RTMR system. Such transformation of processes must not be viewed as a one-time event. The evolution to becoming an increasingly real-time organization is a long-term process that should be addressed through a series of incremental programs. Continually identifying and implementing incremental and sometimes radical innovations should become an ongoing business practice. Considering that competitors will be continually exerting efforts to unseat a company's market position, there is not an ultimate finish line as much as a continual transformation process.

Using a Process Lever: Review Current Steps and Make Modifications

One approach to transforming a process is to review the current steps and then simply make modifications to them. For example, within a process, one or more steps could be merged so that two activities are accomplished simultaneously. A process could also be improved by dividing a single step into separate steps so that additional concepts can be included in the flow (e.g., adding an additional quality check or integrating a new feature to the product at that point in time). Perhaps the improvement calls for changing some aspect of the step, such as converting to a new and more advanced tool, or rearranging the steps of the process.

As an illustration of the step-wise nature of a product process, consider the following example:

Step 1: Customers make use of an online shopping application when they know what they intend to buy. First customers open and initiate the application (which is assumed to exist on a cloud server and the computer/smartphone is providing application access). Once customers have entered the application, it presents a virtual store that allows them to browse the goods. Customers have the option to limit the products presented to those currently available in the inventory of the local store or alternatively the store's complete inventory, including the products at a central warehouse. The application also supports an order history function to permit customers to recall prior orders that they may wish to replicate.

Step 2: Once they are done browsing inventory and prior orders, customers select products and place them in the shopping cart. After opting to check out, they can review the shopping cart contents to verify the desired type, quantity, and price of the products they are interested in. They then choose whether they wish to pick up the purchased items at the local store, have the products shipped by the default shipping process, or request expedited shipping. Once customers confirm the contents of the shopping cart, they enter any optional promotional codes and click on the order button.

Step 3: After a customer has created an order, the application might ask if the customer is a new or returning customer. A returning customer would be asked to enter a user ID and password so the system can associate the current order with the customer's prior orders. If the customer is new, the system could ask the customer to enter personal contact information, including name, email, and phone number, which allows the company to reach out if ordering problems arise or if the customer wants to be notified about future product sales. The application might give the customer the option to save the order to facilitate ordering of future purchases.

Step 4: Once the order has been confirmed, it is summarized and totaled before the customer is allowed to select the desired form of payment. As a further verification of the order, the customer is shown pictures along with a brief description of the selected items. In this example, the customer can specify special handling instructions (e.g., whether the order should be flagged as a gift, etc.). Upon finishing the confirmation, the customer clicks the submit button.

The process changes below show examples of levers that a company can use in its desire to provide a better real-time customer experience:

Option 1. When the company analyzes historic purchasing behaviors, it recognizes that some products are frequently purchased in tandem with other products the store has available. The company determines that one way to improve the customer's real-time experience would be to recommend additional products to the customer based on the decision to purchase a specific product already in the shopping cart. Putting these associated recommendations in front of the customer would save the customer from having to browse for those products. It could also keep the customer from visiting another store. In some instances it could also save the customer from receiving the purchased product only to discover that an associated but independent product is required to facilitate use of the received product.

Option 2. Part of becoming a real-time company implies that a company understands that customers want to know when an ordered product will be delivered so they can plan their time accordingly. If product delivery has been scheduled for a certain date, the company can inform the customer of the expected delivery date. That will allow the customer to use the intervening time productively. By posting an estimated delivery time in the order confirmation, the customer is freed to pursue other interests while awaiting product delivery. The customer can also be given the option to receive ongoing notifications as the order is tracked through the delivery process.

Option 3. By analyzing historic purchases for a specific customer, the company is able to forecast future needs for product consumables. For example, a company might understand that a customer places an order for additional printer paper every month and that the same customer places an order for printer toner every six months. As an aid to the customer, the company can allow the customer to place a scheduled standing order so the required consumables will be automatically ordered, saving the customer from having to frequently visit and place additional orders.

Option 4. The company realizes that many of its customers prefer to conduct business with companies that maintain a positive relationship with them long after they have received and placed the product into use. To expand the customer-company relationship, the company could follow up with customers two months after a purchase to gauge satisfaction and offer suggestions on how the product can be used to better serve them.

Option 5. The company can use its RTMR data to determine the expected time for customers to arrive at the local store to collect the products they ordered online. To accelerate the order fulfillment process, the company should assign employees trained to meet customer demand within the expected arrival time. To support the tasks of those employees, the company should ensure that local store inventories are organized to streamline employee access to products. Furthermore, the pickup process should be designed to provide customers with real-time experiences that meet or beat their expectations for the amount and quality of time spent on picking up their orders.

Using the Process Lever: Reinvent Processes, Involve Customers, Use Cross-Functional Teams

Another approach to transforming a process is to ignore the current process steps and imagine the best real-time experience a customer could have when completing the process. This approach has been referred to in various ways, including reinventing processes, zero-based redesign, and starting with a blank slate or a blank sheet of paper.[36] Such a process reinvention begins by envisioning the desired results of the customer experience for a given process. Once the results of the real-time experience have been envisioned and specified, the process is divided into a set of steps and technologies that support the achievement of those results.

As an example of the blank-sheet process, consider the following example:

Step 1: To open a new bank account, a customer first must visit the local branch of the bank and meet with a representative to consider different account options and provide the necessary identification to ensure the account represents a legitimate bank customer.

Step 2: The customer waits in a line to meet with the bank's representative, which is often the branch manager or assistant manager. On average the lines are short, but they can become long during peak times.

Step 3: The customer is walked through the account setup interview where the various accounts are reviewed, identification information is collected and validated, and finally the account is set up.

The process changes below demonstrate examples of levers that a company can employ to provide a better real-time customer experience:

Option 1: The bank finds that to open an account, the bank representative has to interview the customer and fill in forty-five different data fields before the new account can be opened. The bank starts over with a blank sheet and discovers that a new account can be opened with as few as fifteen fields. When the bank compares this blank-sheet approach to the established processes, it finds that ten fields are never used once the account is opened, ten fields can be populated from outside online sources, and ten more fields can be eliminated by making changes to other long-established banking processes. If the bank reduces the account opening process from forty-five questions to fifteen, customers will likely respond positively because the time savings would mean less time spent with the bank representative; furthermore, the bank representative would be able to support more customers, thereby reducing the time customers spend in the queue.

Option 2: The bank understands that when customers seek to open a new account, they especially dislike having to sit in the lobby while waiting for the bank representative to become free. The bank also understands that many new customers first stand in line to see a teller before they are directed to the representative for an interview. If the bank trained and authorized the tellers to open new bank accounts, the time spent waiting for a bank representative would be reduced.

Option 3: Though the process of opening a new account does require that a bank representative validate customer identification documents, the bank accepts that if a new customer were to enter information online (either from a mobile phone while in the lobby or from a computer prior to visiting the bank), the time spent with the bank representative would be reduced to mere minutes.

The examples above, although realistic, are not intended to represent any specific bank. They do represent options intended to make improvements in the customer's real-time interactions with the company. Making a change to customer interaction processes can provide significant real-time value enhancements, but it is notoriously difficult to develop customer-friendly user interfaces. The realization of user-friendly software is a subjective art. Kanban and agile design philosophies employ customer advisory teams and focus groups in an effort to achieve an optimal user interface. Because customers are directly involved in the design process, these same customers can often provide feedback on the real-time savings associated with a specific design option. Moreover, because these philosophies are incremental in nature and encourage the development of prototype user interfaces that can be evaluated by real customers, each prototype evaluation session provides an opportunity for customers to directly voice an opinion about the potential time savings that each option represents.

As an example, consider the case where a Latin American bank consulted customers for advice at every stage of a customer-driven redesign of the process for opening new accounts.[37] The customer-advisors were first shown sketches of various solutions so they could prioritize the bank's efforts in a way that reflected customer perceptions. An early prototype included a recommendation engine that asked customers questions on their banking patterns and then recommended a specific account type based on their answers. During testing, it became clear that customers almost always wanted to compare account types rather than just accept the recommended type. Thus, the questions asked by the recommendation engine provided little incremental value to the customer real-time experience and, in fact, extended the account setup time longer than was necessary. Based on customer involvement, the solution was redesigned. The recommendation engine with its questions became an option rather than part of the normal flow of the process. With customers' direct involvement with the development team, the bank could be confident that the resulting new customer experience would be acceptable when the updated user system was launched.

Beyond involving customers, organizations should consider establishing a strong cross-functional team to evaluate potential real-time transformational levers. A team made up of experts from different functional areas within the company must have the ability to determine when a proposed transformational lever will increase the complexity of other processes at play. If a transformational lever makes one process more efficient while making others more cumbersome, the value of the transformation could easily be undermined.

Using another banking example, a long-established bank determined it could open a new customer account based on customer input of four critical data fields. This is a significant step forward from banks requiring forty-five, thirty-five, or even fifteen data fields. However, the proposed collection of such a limited amount of data upon account opening meant that other processes in the bank (e.g., compliance) would need to independently gather additional data. The bank needed to decide whether to extend customer time in the account opening process or add customer time in other processes needing additional data. A cross-functional team could provide an informative evaluation of these alternatives.

Innovation is difficult because it requires a change from an established process. As a normal practice, people are generally resistant to change where an established process is working. Although many people will accept that processes can be improved after adoption of an innovation, they also understand that a new process carries some risk that it might compromise the effectiveness associated with the legacy process. Fear of failure may, thus, drive risk-avoidance behavior even when risks can be managed. An important driver of a real-time organization, though, is the realization that a lack of customer-focused real-time innovation carries with it a significant risk of competitive obsolescence.

Becoming Adept at Collaborative Innovation

The Marshall School of Business at the University of Southern California (USC) is the home of the Institute for Communication Technology Management (CTM). CTM is an industry-funded think tank that considers how technology impacts markets and business processes. CTM research projects have focused on mechanisms that drive collaborative innovation for business entities. Its efforts to understand the importance of information systems (IS) personnel to the collaborative innovation process are particularly relevant for digital transformation programs. Further, the adoption of open innovation methodologies, which encourage collaboration with external parties, also plays a significant role in enabling innovation. Research on both these topics, presented below, is relevant for using the process lever to become a more real-time organization.

Collaborative Innovation of Functional Area Personnel with IS Personnel—A USC Marshall Research Project[38]

Collaboration between professionals with different areas of expertise, different motivations, and potentially different employers makes it possible to develop and implement innovations that are more comprehensive than more targeted innovation efforts. Collaborative functional specialists and IS personnel involved in an innovation program are expected to bring a variety of knowledge, skills, and abilities when they join a cross-functional innovation team. Each member of the cross-functional team plays a different role in the innovation program. For example, the project champion would take the lead in advocating for the innovation within the company, whereas other members could serve as targeted specialists. Generally speaking, functional specialists are expected to understand a functional role within the company, whereas the participating IS personnel are expected to understand the nature of digital technology and information flows within the company.

To better understand situations where collaborative innovation would occur, CTM asked corporate leaders to rate their organizations' level of innovation and identify whether the IS function was viewed as a cost of doing business, an enabler of greater efficiency and service, or a strategic partner. The expectation was that innovative organizations would be more likely to view the IS function as a strategic partner. The results confirmed that expectation. Furthermore, CTM found that although some companies consider themselves to be driven primarily by innovation, more companies are driven by a desire to respond to the market, such as customer needs or competitive threats. Firms successfully competing primarily on the basis of innovation are rare (one in fifteen).

Organizations where the IS function is a strategic partner should have IS and functional area staff working collaboratively throughout the innovation process as coequal partners. Besides bringing expertise in their own areas, IS and functional area personnel must also bring an appreciation and understanding of the other area. For example, IS personnel must earn their right to participate in the discussion by bringing an awareness of the organization's mission and current functional area practices/processes along with a deep understanding of how digital assets are tied to the support of those processes. Each member of these collaborative innovation teams needs to be able to look beyond parochial departmental needs to understand the larger role the organization is trying to fulfill. Leaders who want collaborative innovation to succeed must, therefore, prepare people to innovate collaboratively and, as needed, provide appropriate resources. From a long-run perspective, this implies the need to provide opportunities for individuals to be educated and practice collaborative innovation at all levels within the organization, starting with small projects and progressing to more complex ones.

Evolution of the Relationship between IS and Functional Areas in a Large Retail Firm[39]

Consider the case where a large fashion retail firm established a separate, autonomous e-commerce division to develop online sales processes to augment its brick-and-mortar presence. This retail company originally decided to spin off its online processes into an autonomous entity for fear that the online entity would be slowed if it were forced to conform to the processes established to support a physical store. The segmented operations structure worked. Once the e-commerce entity matured, the executive team decided to integrate it back into the parent company so the divisions could jointly tackle the cross-channel integration challenges faced by a multichannel organization.

Reintegrating the e-commerce IS team, which had adopted agile practices, with the traditional corporate IS function allowed the company to transfer technological knowledge, competencies, cultural aspects, and working methodologies. As a result, the merged IS department is more agile and responsible for both online and off-line channels. A steering committee was created that consisted of IS representatives and business stakeholders to govern ongoing projects and prioritize future projects. In addition, "agile boards" were formed for all IS projects.

When the separate e-commerce division was created, leaders understood it to be a real-time product delivery engine unencumbered by legacy processes. The leaders recognized that IS and functional area personnel needed this separate, supportive environment to develop effective collaborative innovation. After reintegration, the process of collaborative innovation developed in the separate e-commerce division was introduced to those in the former brick-and-mortar division to make their work more real time. The IS and functional area personnel with collaborative innovation experience could provide the education and guidance needed to develop effective real-time collaborative innovation throughout the integrated business.

Open Innovation—A USC Marshall Research Project [40]

Open innovation (OI) is an initiative that employs know-how and capabilities of external partners as a key component of a firm's larger innovation effort. Rather than innovation occurring exclusively from within, the firm opens its boundaries to collaborate with external partners. Companies can seek to partner with others under various forms of private and public consortiums. A company can be involved in many such OI efforts where the mission is shared among potential partners that include users, suppliers, competitors, entrepreneurs/start-ups, and universities.

OI can be employed in a variety of contexts, e.g., when collaborating teams are in different parts of the world, such as the US and Europe, or when collaborating teams come from both the public and private sectors. Further, OI can be utilized to create or improve either products or services. The concept of open innovation has evolved and grown significantly over the last couple of decades. Indeed, some view OI as the key to a growth strategy.[41] Given that OI has been used successfully in a variety of contexts, organizational leaders would be wise to ask themselves, "How could we use OI to improve our existing innovation efforts?"

Open innovation requires trust and sharing of information between different companies involved in the same ecosystem. A major challenge for each participating company is to avoid becoming overly dependent on one or more external parties for its essential innovations. Dependence on such parties could be potentially disastrous if those parties fail. To establish alternative paths to success, a company should participate in open innovation relationships with more than one party and limit how much it relies on them for its essential innovations.

Assuming the other OI participants are also collaborating with multiple parties, some of a company's shared data may find its way to an unintended competitor. A potential solution is to establish an exclusive and explicit relationship with a single collaborator. However, that precludes collaboration with other desirable companies.

This USC Marshall study examined factors contributing to OI success. OI adoption is more likely in larger firms that have other resources that allow differentiation from the other OI partners. Non-adopters often raise concerns as an explanation for their nonparticipation, especially over losing core assets and intellectual property (IP). Self-reported data suggests that among OI adopters, revenue growth, profit growth, and innovation capability exceeds that of non-adopters. These results suggest that such cooperative development arrangements create a positive innovation climate. Collaborating with external parties is not necessarily going to be an effective contributor to every firm's innovation programs; nevertheless, many firms have adopted OI and are witnessing positive results from such efforts.

Example of Collaborative Innovation through Open Innovation[42]

In the evolution of hybrid electric drivetrain technology in the automotive industry, the early leader group was comprised of Toyota, Honda, and Ford. The laggard group was composed of General Motors (GM), DaimlerChrysler, and BMW, who joined efforts in an open innovation alliance to catch up to the knowledge frontier. The common goal of overcoming laggard status served as a unifying framework for cooperative R&D. The main reason for them to partner was to spread the risk of large investments in an unestablished—but emerging—technology. Interestingly, however, the alliance partners brought different resources to the table. Whereas GM brought its inventors into the alliance, BMW and DaimlerChrysler primarily brought in funding. Though touted as an "alliance of equals," the allies' contributions were complementary rather than similar.

Though collaborating with competitors inevitably carries with it the fear of opportunism and knowledge breaches, these concerns can be outweighed by the fear of simply falling too far behind in what could be the industry-shaping technology space. According to Peter Savagian, director at GM, "competition between the companies was less important than the challenge of getting a new product to market quickly."

After roughly six years, and having produced 115 patents, the alliance was dissolved in 2011. GM directly utilized the developed technology in its Chevrolet Volt plug-in hybrid. At the termination of the alliance, DaimlerChrysler indicated it would focus on modular hybrid building blocks with scalable lithium-ion batteries. These hybrid building blocks included technologies developed in a separate collaboration with BMW for the Mercedes S-class and BMW 7 Series sedans.

The collaborative innovators sought to reduce the time to develop hybrid electric drivetrain technology that would be part of any new automobile with that industry-shaping technology. Being able to develop that technology as quickly as competitors would allow them to incorporate it into their product design and production processes, allowing them to remain in the mix of real-time hybrid electric automobile producers.

Key Takeaways

- Organizational leaders who seek to guide their organizations toward becoming more real time will find that the process lever is a powerful tool in their toolbox. Processes represent the activities that customers, employees, suppliers, and other stakeholders complete throughout the life of a product or service. Examples of two processes include producing a product and using the product. Within each process are a series of detailed steps. Each of the steps in every process represents a potential core lever to be optimized in an effort to transform an organization to become a real-time organization.

- Process-related levers for transformation include the procedures, physical resources, and personnel used for each step. In the digital age, these levers include digital interfaces and the information and communication technology (ICT) system connected to the interfaces.

- Leaders of real-time organizations regularly specify, develop, and implement process innovations with the goal of valuing customer time more than competitors do.

- Using the process lever, invent a new process or transform an existing process. One approach to transformation is to reinvent an existing process from scratch, similar to inventing a new process. Another approach is to make modifications to the existing process, such as merging one or more steps, dividing a single step into separate steps, rearranging the steps, or changing the way one or more steps are completed.

- In any approach to process design or transformation, ask, "How will the new or revised steps, including changes to the process-related levers, provide a better real-time customer experience?" To develop and evaluate the feasibility and potential success of a transformation, consider involving customers and a strong cross-functional team.

- Organizational leaders should provide an environment where employees and other stakeholders can become adept at collaborative innovation. In this age of digital transformations, corporate leaders who view the IS function as a strategic partner will want to develop their process innovations in collaboration with IS personnel. Furthermore, leaders seeking to foster a climate of innovation should consider collaborating with external partners on open innovation projects. Even if those projects are not focused on transforming processes, employees participating in those projects would gain experience that could be applied to process innovations.

- Many potential innovations could use the process lever, but organizations have limited resources. Business leaders are responsible for identifying and prioritizing the process innovations to implement. These decisions and assignment of the organization's limited resources to specific transformational programs should be aided by data from the RTMR system. More specifically, those who are involved in making process improvement recommendations should review data on the real-time experiences of customers who have interacted with the company and its products or services. Process innovations that are implemented should address problems or opportunities revealed by analysis and interpretation of the RTMR data.

- Organizations leading the real-time revolution will have the agility to detect and respond to changing customer real-time expectations more rapidly than competitors.

Chapter

6

Using the Real-Time Data Lever to Transform to a More Real-Time Organization

Netflix is one of the great transformational success stories in the history of entertainment. What had been a customer base of 20 million subscribers a few years ago, mainly in the US, is now more than 120 million subscribers around the world. What began as a logistics-based entertainment company that shipped physical DVDs has evolved into a massive digital entertainment empire. Netflix now dominates the video subscription market.[43]

Netflix tracks what people watch and is able to utilize that data to predict interest in other content. As an objective, Netflix strives to provide entertainment content for all viewers. The data that Netflix has amassed continues to grow, allowing the company to get better at personalizing recommendations in an effort to increase a customer's engagement. The Netflix service structure also allows the company to understand how viewing habits shift as people move from one viewing device to another. For example, Netflix knows what device the customer is using to begin watching certain content; it can tell when the customer pauses, fast-forwards, rewinds, or moves to a new device to continue watching that content. This knowledge is the source of competitive advantage in that it shapes the way Netflix negotiates content licensing deals. The data is a proprietary component of its strategy, and only a small portion of that insight is ever shared. It also allows Netflix to focus its content curation efforts to the desires of an individual customer.

For Netflix, it is the data that makes the difference and drives the company's larger strategy.[44]

The success of Netflix is a testament to its effort to be a real-time company. The data collected allows it to negotiate for content that customers value and provides the vehicle that allows it to serve the content to the customer in a personalized manner that makes it easy to wade through a large content library. As a result, Netflix provides better real-time experiences than competitors, which has fueled its rapid customer growth. Netflix understands that it must continue to improve the customer experience or emerging competitors will attract its customers.

Real-time data is an essential component throughout the real-time company's processes. For example, completion of an online order process requires data about the product ordered, the customer, and the method of payment. Google and other search engines use data derived from customer searches to support the process of displaying ads that are related to those searches and, thus, are likely to be of interest to customers. Once the customer has used the search engine to find a store that carries a product of interest, the customer can link directly to the online retailer of interest. Amazon and other online retailers use the data they collect while the customer is browsing their stores to highlight best sellers and products likely to be of personal interest to the customer.

As these real-time companies collect data about customer behaviors, that data is saved in their version of an RTMR system. Depending on the company, the data can include start and stop times of customer-centric processes, resources consumed, and customer satisfaction. After collecting data, organizations must then employ it to drive business value for the company; whereas data that drives business advantage is extremely valuable, data that does not drive incremental value for the company has little value. Real-time companies, companies that understand the value their customers place on their time, will treat the data in their RTMR systems as an asset, information that has the potential to further improve their ability to serve their customers. The value of these data assets is realized when the company uses the data to surpass competitors' ability to demonstrate respect for the customer's use of time.

Real-time data often supports agility in the quest to value customer time. It supports faster customization or completion of operational processes. Analysis of real-time data also provides the basis for a company to rapidly identify priorities for improving customer real-time experiences and to rapidly innovate to solve lingering customer issues or emerging opportunities. Although the establishment of an RTMR system will take time, the investment will increase the company's agility, thereby making it possible to be more efficient as it progresses along the real-time continuum. The RTMR system becomes a platform that, once established, allows the company to focus on customer needs in a way that customers recognize as faster or more satisfying. Adopting a real-time philosophy, where a company values the customer's time better than competitors do, requires an investment of company time to develop the requisite understanding of the customer's time experiences throughout the life of the company's products and services. Once the RTMR system is established, it is an investment that pays large dividends. Organizational leaders should ask this important question: "Have we invested in an RTMR system that collects data reflecting a real-time philosophy?"

Enabling the Use of the Real-Time Data Lever— Addressing Security and Privacy Concerns

The internet, and technology in general, has made it easier to amass a wealth of data about customers. This wealth of information can be extremely valuable when trying to understand customers, including the way they buy, use, and maintain products or services. Assembling such a large store of data, although a valuable asset for the company, creates new risks. Recent events in the news demonstrate the risks that occur when a company fails to protect these assets. To deal with these risks, companies have developed robust policies and practices that address data security and privacy concerns.

Addressing Security and Privacy Concerns— The Mohegan Sun Example[45]

The culture of surveillance and accountability is innate at Mohegan Sun, the world's second-largest casino (measured by number of games and square footage), owned by the Mohegan Tribal Gaming Authority, with $1.4 billion in annual revenues. The casino operation at the heart of Mohegan Sun collects an enormous amount of data from its customers, some three million of whom have volunteered their identifying information—names, addresses, emails, and such—in order to join its Player's Club affinity-and-rewards program. About three-quarters of Mohegan Sun's gaming business comes from "carded play"—that is, people using Player's Club cards to earn and track points. Some regulars literally attach themselves to slot machines and gaming tables by hooking their Player's Club cards to their belt loops with plastic cords; they insert the cards in an electronic card-reader and sit physically tethered to the gambling equipment. Psychologically, these customers have bound themselves to the casino, and as a result the casino has found that these customers spend more time at the casino when they could stray to the nearby Foxwoods Resort Casino or elsewhere. But collecting data on customers' gambling habits is a delicate issue, particularly in a business where expectations of privacy are so strong. That's why Mohegan Sun's customer data is kept at an off-site facility that provides both physical and electronic protection systems that are more secure than many banks.

The combination of rewards from carded play and data security has enabled Mohegan Sun to collect data on the gambling habits of some three million customers with the full endorsement of its customer base. Mohegan Sun's experience with customers voluntarily providing their data indicates that customers are interested in a data-enhanced real-time experience. But the customer endorsement of the program demands that the company can demonstrate that it is able to protect the data required to drive the experience.

Organizations collect a lot of data directly from customers, much of it in exchange for some incentive or benefit, such as a coupon, warranty, loyalty rewards, announcements about new products, and sales events. Customers expect companies to adequately protect their data with security procedures. In general, customers often consider their use of a product or service a private matter; however, they are willing to share their data with companies they trust in the belief that the company will use the information to improve current and future products and services. The willingness of customers to share data with a company is based on the level of trust and respect that has been earned between the customer and the company. The greater the level of trust, the more a customer is willing to share. Should something happen to negatively impact the level of trust between a company and a customer, the customer will likely cease sharing data with that company. Moreover, simply because a customer shares data with one company does not mean that the customer will be willing to share the same data with another company. In many cases, when it has been discovered that a company has shared its customer data with a partner that is untrusted by the customer, the customer recourse is to punish the parent company by terminating their business relationship.

Addressing Security and Privacy of Customer Data—A USC Marshall Research Project[46]

A general customer data problem that organizations face as they engage in transformations using the real-time data lever is what to do with regard to security and privacy of customer data. This includes policies that call for sharing customer data with partners. Many customers will share what they consider to be private personal data with a trusted company that they have engaged with. If the customers consider their data private, they do not want the trusted collecting company to share the data with others unless they are asked to consider whether that partner company is also trusted. Before sharing the data with its partners, a real-time company will seek the permission of its customers and explain the need, or they will implicitly take on the responsibility to ensure the partner companies have established protocols to protect the data. In the end, trust is a corporate characteristic, and when it is extended to a network of partners, the level of trust is determined by the weakest link in the system of partners. A real-time company understands that although data is an enabler that allows the company to act in real time, the tools needed to face the heightened security and privacy risks associated with the data are a prerequisite. This USC Marshall research has found that companies that are leaders in securing their customer data and properly balancing customer privacy concerns with data sharing grow revenues and profits faster than companies that are average or below.

Government and regulatory institutions typically focus on issues that have created wide-scale community concern. Efforts from these sectors generally seek to establish rules and procedures that prevent the reoccurrence of legacy faults. In contrast, real-time companies seeking to be leaders strive to go beyond minimal legal requirements in an effort to provide their customers with better experiences. For example, the legal community has defined personally identifiable information (PII) to include telephone number, home address, birthdate, Social Security number, credit card number, birthplace, and driver's license number. Many legal authorities press to ensure that all companies take steps to protect PII data. In contrast, a real-time company will establish protections beyond the minimum and provide enhanced levels of security and privacy related to not only PII data but also other data that the customer considers sensitive.

For example, a health-care company might treat biometric data collected via the Internet of Things (IoT) as sensitive data even if it is not linked to an individual's PII. In this case, the company recognizes that the biometric data in itself is anonymous, but once it is linked to a set of records that detail device ownership, the sensitivity of the data is significantly increased. If the data is hacked or inadvertently placed on a jump drive that is later misplaced, the repercussions could be enormous. In an effort to minimize risks, this example health-care company can encrypt the health-care data so that if it were linked to PII data and then lost, impacts would be reduced.

Real-time companies that outperform others manage security and privacy by paying attention to technology, design, and people. From the technology perspective, technology in the area of security is making constant gains, so companies must actively manage upgrades. From the design perspective, security and privacy cannot be treated as an afterthought. Preventive measures must be designed into the system at the onset. From the human perspective, regardless of how good the design and technology are, if personnel are not trained to prevent threats, identify threats, and act on threats, systems will be compromised. Real-time companies display heightened awareness of technology (encryption, authentication, data segmentation, firewalls, etc.); design of controls for data confidentiality, integrity, and availability; and the need for human preparedness (such as training, preparedness drills, and escalation procedures).

Many companies ask external experts to assess whether their level of protection is sufficient and conduct internal risk analysis to determine if the risk justifies incremental investments. As a part of these audits, some companies use penetration testing to evaluate their security efforts to protect the privacy of customer data. Given that new threats are constantly emerging, it is impossible to avoid all potential breaches; therefore, real-time companies utilize these regular audit programs to test and evaluate threat response procedures. The response procedures can be much more involved than the detection/protection procedures because they can involve personnel from IT, legal, marketing, strategy, management, and others. For some companies these procedures can include notifying impacted customers as soon as possible after a breach is detected, whereas other companies might wait until the threat is understood and contained. Though some argue in favor of a simplistic threat response protocol, it is clear that the response must reflect the nature of the data in jeopardy and the nature of the attack. More research in the area of customer-experience response protocols is clearly needed.

Interestingly, this USC Marshall research has demonstrated that successful companies often intentionally "advertise" their data protection policies to their customers. The positive impact of such programs is to educate customers about the nature of the collected data and the efforts to secure the data. These efforts, which may be part of a company's real-time philosophy, are intended not only to create trust but also to minimize the loss of trust when adverse situations occur. Apple is an example of a company that has touted its commitment to the protection of individual data.

"Advertising" Apple's Privacy Policy[47]

According to Business Insider, "Apple is increasingly highlighting its pro-privacy policies." The Verge reports that Apple CEO Tim Cook, speaking at a privacy conference in Brussels, "gave an impassioned and forceful speech. He reiterated familiar talking points like Apple's commitment to privacy (and, by implication, its rivals' lack of commitment) while spelling out public concerns in recent years regarding data collection, surveillance, and manipulation." On Apple's updated privacy website, it states, "We're committed to keeping your personal information safe. That's why we innovate ways to safeguard your privacy on your device, why we're up front about how we personalize your experience, and why we equip developers with the best tools to protect your data."

Many companies have taken the path of aggregating data before sharing it with partners. This further obscures PII specifics from the partners; effectively, the companies are creating a new, non-customer-specific data set from customer data. Given that this new data set is not customer-specific, the data can be shared without customer approval; however, some companies ask their customers to approve such sharing, whereas others post descriptive information about their data sharing policies in an effort to be transparent. In contrast, the less successful companies share data without any acknowledgment of their data sharing practices. To be clear, data sharing is not a bad thing; in fact, companies that share data with their partners tend to outperform companies that prevent data sharing. The point, however, is that the real-time company is ideally transparent about its data sharing policies, whereas the required level of transparency is driven by the competitive market and the customer.

Data security can be defined as the effort employed by a company to ensure the data is used only for the company's intended purposes. In contrast, data privacy means a company will only use customer data as the customer intended. Data can be secure but not private, or it can be private but not secure. Research in this project indicates that the most successful companies allow customers to establish personal data sharing profiles with defaults that reflect their desires. When customers are allowed to increase or relax privacy settings to reflect their personal preferences, they feel they are a respected part of the conversation and are encouraged to share more.

Addressing Employee Concerns Regarding Knowledge Sharing—A USC Marshall Research Project[48]

In addition to collecting customer data, companies collect considerable data about their employees to support basic business functions, such as payroll, evaluations, and more. Many companies go beyond the collection of basic operational data to include employee input on improving task performance or process efficiencies. Employees who provide such input contribute to understanding best practices, methodologies, and on-the-job experiences. Knowledge sharing is a term used to describe voluntary employee participation in this data collection and interpretation process. Although knowledge sharing is often associated with positive outcomes (e.g., better learning, coordination, efficiency, and work quality), it can cause angst among the employees as well.

Knowledge Sharing at Caterpillar[49]

Caterpillar is the world's leading manufacturer of earthmoving machinery. The organization's vision and mission for knowledge sharing, developed with input from more than one hundred community managers, is to be a global leader whose productivity and competitive advantage are maximized because validated, up-to-date knowledge is freely and easily shared across the value chain. Members of the global value chain include joint venture affiliations, retirees, suppliers, dealers, and customers. The stated mission for knowledge sharing at Caterpillar is to provide efficient, reliable, and easy access to knowledge and collaboration with others across the value chain for the purpose of performance improvement. Caterpillar's culture drives employees to be open and willing to share across the value chain with a high level of trust. Caterpillar has found that people do not share information with other people whom they do not trust.

Caterpillar's Knowledge Network and communities of practice have been very effective knowledge-sharing tools for the organization. The Knowledge Network is a tool that was developed in-house and continuously evolves as the business changes. Originally the tool was not easy to use. The interface was redesigned for usability to address employees' fears that were creating barriers to knowledge sharing, including concerns of looking foolish. The Knowledge Network is a "right now" tool to help people get the information they need right away to help them do their jobs effectively. The organization uses a delegated community management process. The community managers determine if external value chain partners and joint ventures have access.

There are no explicit rewards or incentives for participating or collaborating via the Knowledge Network, so the activity must have some intrinsic value related to what participants are evaluated on (their job or business process). If being in a community of practice is not providing value as it relates to their business objectives and annual performance, people will "cut and run" because they won't waste time posting and browsing.

If employees do not trust the employer or coworkers, they will be more reluctant to participate in voluntary programs, and they will resent technology-enabled monitoring programs. Lack of participation not only impedes a company's ability to gather the data to improve operations, it can also trigger an avoidance mechanism on the part of the employees, which weakens the processes the company was hoping to improve. Thus, unless the efforts at knowledge sharing are supported by the employee base, those efforts are doomed. Therefore, knowledge sharing and, more generally, collaborating require the employees to understand and appreciate the necessity and value of the collected data; employees must buy into the position that the value of the benefits outweigh the risks associated with the data collection process.

One employee concern is that when employees are competing for raises and promotions, some employees will attempt to game the system and, in so doing, undermine others. If a company creates an environment of fear, where the perceived cost of sharing an idea is more significant than the benefit from sharing, it encourages counterproductive behavior, such as withholding knowledge. In contrast, an environment of trust encourages increased knowledge sharing.

In the internet age, many employees are concerned about the privacy of their personal information that is disseminated out on the internet. Similarly, they are also concerned about the privacy of personal data, including knowledge, that they share with their companies. When employees are concerned about their employer's use of their private data, it implies the employees do not trust their employers to keep their data secure. It could also imply the employees do not understand how a company uses its employee data. When a real-time company is dealing with customer data, it must demonstrate a respect for the customer's time and an ability to protect the data. Likewise, the company must accept that there is an equally valuable relationship between the employee and the company. If the company fails to demonstrate respect for the employee's use of time or if it fails to protect the employee's data, efforts to improve corporate operations may be stymied.

Companies demonstrating greater care in safeguarding company data, which includes both employee and customer data, are more likely to have established greater trust with employees and customers. At the same time, greater security measures suggest that it is important to be wary of others seeking to obtain and use the data illicitly for their advantage. The research results suggest that greater wariness in conjunction with greater security contribute to success.

When addressing privacy and knowledge sharing concerns, organizational leaders should strive for both trust and wariness in their employees. Employee trust is necessary to encourage knowledge sharing. Wariness is necessary for employees to take security measures seriously and safeguard data. Finding the balance that encourages sharing and safeguarding data at the same time is the challenge.

Addressing Employee Concerns Regarding Knowledge Sharing—The HP Analytics Example[50]

Employee fears about sharing their knowledge have been widely recognized. Building a culture that overcomes this fear is essential, but it is a journey of many steps. HP Analytics is an example of an organization that began small and continually adapted its approach to knowledge sharing. HP Analytics' employees work in teams that provide support to various HP business units. They are tasked with creating insights out of data; it is a knowledge development process. Leadership at HP Analytics recognizes that its success depends on its ability to collaborate and amalgamate insights to create new knowledge and has publically recognized this fact.

> *"Our whole business is about developing knowledge, and if we do not manage our knowledge well, we end up re-inventing the wheel; we end up not doing the task efficiently."*

The key to harnessing knowledge for maximum benefit is to develop a knowledge sharing culture within the organization. However, employees often consider their personal knowledge as their key competitive asset and may be reluctant to share it for fear of losing their competitive edge. Efforts to employ technology to foster a collaborative environment cannot by themselves create a knowledge sharing culture. Though collaborative tools can facilitate sharing, deliberate and planned initiatives are required to change employees' behavior before a knowledge sharing culture will be adopted.

HP Analytics has learned that fostering a knowledge sharing culture requires many targeted actions that can be divided into three categories—platform, people, and process.

Platform

- Use easily available and scalable web-based collaborative technologies
- Support the online platform with off-line initiatives

People

- Communicate knowledge sharing objectives
- Make knowledge sharing fun

- Appoint appropriate knowledge management ambassadors
- Focus on middle management to secure buy-in

Process

- Start small
- Brand and market the knowledge management program
- Adopt multilevel metrics with alignment of goals for different levels
- Publicize knowledge sharing behaviors
- Reinvent the knowledge management program
- Replicate the knowledge management program

When sharing these activity plans with employees, HP Analytics' leaders emphasized that knowledge management was a process—a journey—and not a one-time project. It was more of a philosophy, a way of operating a business. For the company to benefit, the employees must embrace it, continuously improve it, be creative in its positioning, and constantly reinvent it.

HP Analytics illustrates an incremental, continuous-improvement approach to knowledge management that can be applied in real-time organizations. Using knowledge management as part of a real-time data lever would be guided by a priority of valuing customer time more effectively than competitors do. For example, the knowledge sharing objectives (under People above) would be guided by this priority, as would the goals for different levels (under Process above).

Enabling the Use of the Real-Time Data Lever— What Is Required to Convert Data to Business Value

Today's business leaders live in a data-rich era. Business leaders have access to large amounts of data (structured and unstructured), including data about corporate operations, individual customers, and competitors. The volume of data being collected is expanding at an unprecedented rate. Real-time organizations are constantly facing the issue of how to turn this large volume of data into incremental business value. What are successful companies doing to convert data to business value?

Converting Data to Business Value— Bank of America Example[51]

Cathy Bessant, chief operations and technology officer of Bank of America, reported that her company looks at the process of creating incremental value from the data they collect as an ongoing process. They look at data as one of their most important resources. This data forms the basis for their efforts to changes products, identify new opportunities, improve customers' lives, change economies, and in general make things better. Achieving these goals has called for the development of a data architecture, a storage philosophy, a data transportation system, and a data protection system. Building this system was and continues to be challenging. The resulting system has no immediately identifiable business value. Instead, what they have is a system and a methodology where any outcome they wish to consider can be supported by a data-driven analysis. The business value comes from the better decisions their businesses make every day. Bank of America believes they are in their infancy in their efforts to think about how they can employ a wealth of disparate data to drive their mission, a mission that focuses on improving their customers' financial lives.

Bank of America illustrates the importance and scope that the data lever has. It also points out the risk taking needed to invest in building a data lever when the business value cannot necessarily be known in the present. The bank's leaders expect the investment to be justified by future decisions that they believe will significantly improve their customers' financial lives. These characteristics apply to the data lever in real-time organizations. Real-time organizational leaders believe that the investment in the data lever will be significant in transforming the organization to value customer time more effectively than competitors do.

Converting Data to Business Value— A USC Marshall Research Project[52]

At this point, an organizational leader should be asking, "What steps should I be encouraging within our organization to make it possible for us to convert data to business value?" This USC Marshall research provides important insights. It shows that real-time companies are expanding their data analytics teams and providing these teams with even more data. Data analytic teams possess data that describe competitive products and services, market environments, customer comments on social networks, customer data, data about competitors' customers, and revenue and business model data. These data analytic teams split their time between efforts to increase situational awareness, predictive analysis, and market response. Situational awareness seeks to understand what happened and why (e.g., descriptive and diagnostic analytics). Predictive analysis seeks to understand how historic trends serve to forecast future conditions. Market response analysis assumes some action will be taken to continue or change the current trajectory. Prescriptive analytics recommend actions to take. Each of these different types of analytics has the common goal of uncovering some new business insight that can be acted upon in order to improve business performance. It is clear that companies that make significant use of data analytics have a demonstrable competitive advantage.

The highest-performing companies make it clear that it is the talented people and supportive processes that generate business insights from data and drive their business success. A key enabler of success is related to these companies' efforts to include a diversity of perspectives when assembling their analytics teams; different types of people are required to maximize data-driven benefits. One perspective included in these teams represents that of the data scientists, people who have analytical talent and domain expertise. Another perspective included in these teams represents the technologists, who understand how technology generates the data that feeds the analytic systems (and the strengths and weaknesses of such data). There are also business domain specialists, including data-sophisticated managers and analysts, who understand the relationship between data and business processes and how data can create business value. Teams may also involve business domain specialists whose role is to represent the customer, pose the right questions for analysis, and interpret and challenge the results. A data analytics function is important for real-time companies, but such a function would not be complete without supportive processes and people willing to act decisively based upon interpreting the results of analysis. It is what people do with the results from all that data that creates the true value for the business.

As a real-time company assembles its data analytics plan needed to convert the RTMR system data into business insights, it must, at a minimum, include the following:[53]

- Acquire any needed technology

- Establish procedures to collect and store needed data

- Address security and privacy concerns; manage risks while finding the balance between trust and wariness

- Periodically realign organizational strategy and culture to reflect data-driven insights

- Hire or develop data-sophisticated action-driven people with the skills to discover data-driven insights

Key Takeaways

- The technology, data collection procedures, and security and privacy practices that are part of the real-time data lever make it possible to collect data for the RTMR system. The data collected includes not only the data to monitor customer interactions but also all kinds of other data, including typical business performance data, employee data that includes knowledge the employees share, and data on competitors and economic conditions.

- The volume of data available to the real-time organization is rapidly growing and will only accelerate with the advent of the Internet of Things (IoT). Real-time companies must stay on top of managing their data, including their privacy, security, and sharing policies. They will want to avoid being overwhelmed with addressing data issues while also under pressure to compete effectively.

- The data lever includes investments in not only data and technology supporting data collection, analysis, and use but also the supporting personnel and processes. Data analysts, data-sophisticated managers, and others who are part of the real-time data lever make it possible to convert data to business value. They analyze the RTMR data, interpret the results, set priorities for improvement, and respond to the competition by identifying, evaluating, and implementing innovations.

- Organizations that have joined the real-time revolution use their investments in the data lever to transform steps in the life of a product or service to provide customers with real-time experiences that are better than experiences provided by their competitors. Leaders and members in organizations aspiring to be real-time leaders will want to ask, "Have we made investments in collecting, managing, and using data that allow us to become a real-time leader?"

Chapter

7

Using the Real-Time People Lever to Transform to a More Real-Time Organization

Zillow is a market leader for customers searching for real estate. It positions itself as a consumer empowerment agent by providing data on the real estate market and connecting buyers with real estate agents as needed. For sellers, Zillow helps the consumer search through the market to find data that helps them locate desirable properties. It also helps connect various contractors and renters to homeowners. Its rich marketplace of current real estate data is positioned as an aid to consumers, and this community of users allows Zillow to sell advertising software tools to real estate professionals.[54]

By innovating with new product features in response to a changing competitive environment, Zillow has been able to use its product lever to provide better real-time customer experiences for customers and real estate agents alike. These product innovations help make consumers more efficient when purchasing a house and also make real estate agents more efficient in their efforts to support their customers. One of the innovations allowed customers to edit home facts that could affect the Zestimate, Zillow's estimated market value for an individual home. As with many product innovations, people using the product need to learn how to use the new feature. Zillow provides help for both customers and real estate professionals. For customers, Zillow provides links within its website to guide them through updating their home facts and correcting inaccuracies. For real estate professionals, Zillow provides an explanation of how to help guide homeowners through the process in five easy steps that include directions and images of the mobile website at each step.[55]

Zillow has recognized the importance of paying attention to the people lever in making changes. Without appropriate assistance for homebuyers and real estate professionals, a new product feature intended to provide these people with what they wanted could go unused. Even worse, this innovation would lead to negative real-time experiences if users were frustrated by difficulties using it.

All organizations understand that competitive pressures increase over time and they must evolve to survive. When an organization undertakes a transformational program that is intended to make the company more real time by using the people lever, the company must either further develop the existing staff, customers, or relevant others, or it must acquire personnel to fulfill identified resource deficits. It is essential that the adapted or additional resources have the appropriate motivation and correspondingly appropriate knowledge, skills, and abilities (KSAs) to permit the company to move in a new direction. An example of desirable motivation for such resources includes the employees' drive to participate in the company's overarching efforts to value customer time as a precious customer resource. An example of an appropriate KSA is the ability to understand and communicate the business value associated with the company's efforts to improve efficient use of customer time.

It is imperative that employees understand that customer expectations will continue to rise as they place an increased emphasis on their time value and more companies join the real-time revolution. Companies must continually improve performance over time. Employees must accept that what is great responsiveness today will slip to become adequate tomorrow and, ultimately, become unacceptable as competitors improve their responsiveness and customer expectations rise.

For those who are responsible for monitoring and responding to real-time customer experiences, KSAs that are associated with capturing RTMR data may be appropriate. For personnel analyzing RTMR data, appropriate KSAs include the appreciation for how the quality of the experience impacts the value of time. These innovators should have KSAs that reflect an appreciation of the overriding value of time across all of a customer's interactions with the company and its products and services. Properly motivated, these analysts would be tasked with ensuring that an innovative improvement to one aspect of the organization and, ultimately, the customer experience does not cause degradation to another.

It is essential for all employees of a real-time company to understand the role they play in not only serving customers but also going beyond and helping customers make better use of their time. As a nonreplicable resource, time will become increasingly precious as customers continually strive to achieve more in a targeted time span. Customers will increase their appreciation of companies that help them realize their time-driven objectives.

When a company seeks to become more centered on meeting customers' time-driven objectives, it should recognize that its culture will change. The real-time transformation will most likely result in changes in the behavior and attitudes of people, including those within the company and those outside that interact with it. The transformation could be based on training employees to provide faster and more accurate customer service. More generally it could be based on employees developing new knowledge and skills. It could be based on acquiring and using new information and communications technologies or making better use of existing tools, thereby changing how people work and communicate. It could be based on internal process changes that require employees to be trained to perform the new processes appropriately. In other cases it could be based on product changes that impact customers, employees, suppliers, and other stakeholders, requiring training and support to assist them with the changes. All of these changes involve the use of the people lever.

When a company decides to undergo a transformation to provide better real-time customer experiences, it should think carefully about the people affected, the changes in people that are needed, and what will make those changes possible. Some of the people will be those responsible for leading and implementing the change. Others will be those living with the change; they will be participating in the experiences that occur after the transformation. Some people may be part of both groups.

The people lever can be the primary means of transforming the organization to value customer time more effectively than the competition. However, when another lever, such as the product lever, is the primary mechanism to transform the company, a transformation program with human capital as a supporting lever will also probably be needed. It is clear that corporate leaders must play an active role to encourage the company's employees to participate in such a transformational program. What is often overlooked, though, is that these leaders may also need to enlist the support of external stakeholders, including suppliers and possibly even the customers, for such a transformation to reach its full potential. The leadership team, working together, must help all those touched by the changes understand the goal, why it is important, and how their roles in the transformation create a benefit for everyone. When an organization joins the real-time revolution, the messaging emanating from the leaders must reflect the importance the organization places on the value of customer time. A more subtle but important consideration is the fact that the messaging should also reflect management's desire to demonstrate a higher appreciation for customer time than the competition.

Transformations with the people lever run the risk of failure if the proper support is missing. For example, assume your company enhances its product with new features that allow it to better support the product in the field. The customer's perceived value of these features is not in the features themselves but in the more efficient support services that stand behind the product. This perceived value only becomes tangible if the support services personnel are trained to use these new features so customer services are improved. Should these additional features slow the support process due to increased complexity or lack of appropriate training, the effort to improve the product will have negative repercussions.

Similarly, consider the situation where a company enhances a product's features to make customer use more efficient. It then relies upon alternative training materials and methods such as online FAQs (frequently asked questions), digital manuals, or videos to enable customers to learn how to make direct use of these features. These support materials are well intentioned; however, if the content is difficult to find or use, the efficiency improvements provided by the new features are effectively offset by the time needed to find and digest the digital training materials.

As one further example, consider the company that creates an option for customers to share their experiences with a product so other customers can benefit from a larger community of knowledge. Such a well-meaning program is often unappreciated, unless the company provides a participation incentive and curates submittals so they are evaluated for validity and presented in an organized fashion. What could be a great program could end up undermining the larger goal of respecting customer use of time. The company needs to consider the total time and quality of experiences the customer has when dealing with the company and its products and services.

The story of Steris is an example of a company that focused on changing its personnel via training to instill a goal of being more customer service oriented.

Steris[56]

Steris is a global leader in the business of manufacturing sterilization products, surgical equipment, and other medical and laboratory accessories. It maintains operations in more than one hundred countries and has twelve thousand associates worldwide. Steris health-care services emphasize service excellence to differentiate the company from the competition, protect margins, grow revenue, and increase customer loyalty.

Severe market pressures have forced Steris's clients to ask for price and cost reductions while increasing their expectations for higher levels of responsiveness. To address these changes in the market, Steris knew that significant organizational and process changes needed to be considered. Steris began by defining every customer touchpoint as a potential place to drive innovation. For each touchpoint, multiple low-cost action steps were identified and then prioritized based on their ability to lower expenses while enhancing customer experience.

Steris partnered with UP! Your Service (a training company that focuses on direct cultural transformations) to help manage its efforts to instill a shared value of service excellence in its employees. Steris implemented an educational campaign that included:

- Service leadership workshops to identify additional building blocks for improvement

- Town hall events to energize staff and recognize progress

- Creation of a "train the trainer" program where thirty-five workshop leaders were certified to implement service education for one thousand employees

- Creation of a phased action-planning workshop where each phase targeted specific customer-centric improvements. Over the first three years the company was able to drive specific improvements to:

  ▸ Equipment uptime

  ▸ Response time

> ▸ First visit fix rate and total time to repair
>
> ▸ Customer communication
>
> ▸ Customer experience and customer loyalty survey results
>
> Steris did not employ the people lever explicitly to achieve an overarching goal of valuing customer time; however, it did use the people level to identify and prioritize efforts that customers value. The goal of instilling a shared vision that values service excellence resonated among the employees by prioritizing elements that valued customer time, such as improving response time, first visit fix rate, and total time to repair.

Executives may adopt a different approach to developing among employees the overarching goal of valuing customer time better than competitors do. For example, they can intentionally focus on helping employees understand this goal, why it is important, and how they can achieve it as part of their communications via an internal social network.

The story of Degordian is an example of a company that focused on changing its personnel via hiring to provide clients with better quality experiences that meet their time expectations while also satisfying its leaders' goal of growth.

Degordian[57]

Degordian is an independent digital production and marketing agency. As of 2014, it had one hundred employees and four offices, but the story began with two friends. In the first five and a half years, revenues grew from €30,000 to more than €2 million, despite a recession in Croatia with GDP decreasing by 18 percent. CEO Daniel Ackermann attributed the company's success to its focus on the basics: "We . . . always kept our focus on people and the quality of work." And over time, one thing remained the same—the desire to grow.

1. The Beginning (2–10 employees)

Degordian could not afford to hire people with a lot of experience, so it augmented its staff with student-workers who had the drive to learn and develop themselves. This increased level of resource agility often resulted in times when work was completed ahead of schedule. At other times work required days, nights, and weekends to meet deadlines.

2. The Foundation of the Future (10–20 employees)

Growth occurred rapidly.

3. The Wake-Up Call (20–40 employees)

Over time, the company began to attract more and more experts with years of experience. It took on projects that were far more complex than before. Teams of three designers worked together on delivering the best result possible. Capacity and speed increased. With more employees and larger teams, the company could not only take on a larger number of projects, it could also complete projects in a shorter amount of time.

4. The Golden Age (40–80 employees)

At the beginning of each project, the objectives of the client were shared with the entire team so there was a shared understanding of success. Each team implemented a quality assurance process so that clients could be sure that everything delivered was of the highest standard. The teams knew the company collected feedback on client satisfaction and that feedback was shared with the team. According to Ackermann, "Giving our clients the results they want is of the highest importance, so we defined precise project guidelines and tracking mechanisms to additionally boost quality and productivity while keeping a close eye on our finances."

Client feedback showed that Degordian delivered effectively. Because each team was clear on the objectives at the onset and the teams knew that project success would be defined by client feedback, the CEO's remark, "This was by far our finest hour," was a powerful statement. It validated a company culture that focused on creating value for the customer.

But the CEO recognized that implementation of changes slows down as hiring increases the number of employees. Ackermann states: "When extensive changes are to be made, we have to inform and educate a larger number of people, which can take weeks or even months."

Degordian sought to achieve two goals at the same time. Achieving one of those goals—better quality projects that met customer time expectations—helped Degordian become a more real-time organization. Use of the people lever to hire additional expert staff made it possible for Degordian to achieve better quality results. Hiring additional people also made it possible to achieve its other goal of growth. The need for leaders to communicate with organizational members is apparent in the CEO's recognition that extensive changes require more time to inform and educate. Executives should expect to communicate when leading real-time transformations, particularly where the people lever is concerned.

Executive Use of Internal Social Networks— A USC Marshall Research Project

Many companies have undertaken corporate use of internal social networks to support communications by executives, with mixed results. These efforts often include sharing updates and announcements with employees, responding to their questions and concerns, listening to their ideas, and holding conversations with them.[58]

In some cases, these posts can have a very positive impact, as they provide employees with insights into what the executives value individually and as a group. However, if the posts are simply a retransmission of official news and happenings, employees often leap to the conclusion that the rhetoric about sharing and collaboration is nothing more than a "one-way street." If the engagements are focused to a limited number of participants, the employees will not consider the exchanges as reflective of the larger corporate culture. Moreover, if the engagements are not genuine, the effort can actually damage the employee-management trust relationship that is required to maintain a cohesive corporate identity. Executive communication can be a key contributor to shared goals and a positive corporate culture but only when that communication is able to engage the employee as an active partner in a shared endeavor.

A positive corporate culture is created in an environment where the employees feel authenticity, attachment, pride, and fun.[59]

- Authenticity occurs when the words of leaders are aligned with the leaders' personal actions; the leaders are seen to be walking the talk, even when the "talk" refers to interactions on a collaboration site.

- Attachment is a feeling among employees that they belong to a community of shared values and interests, a community focused on common objectives. The most successful companies are those that are able to activate an entire organization around a common mission.

- Pride is a belief that the company values are recognized externally by the public and that internally the employees are recognized for their contribution to that achievement; employees who feel their contribution to the larger mission is unappreciated rapidly disconnect.

- Fun is not the same as entertaining; fun is the feeling of playfulness that employees feel when experimenting with new ideas at work.

The content of executive communication must reinforce these four elements of a positive corporate culture. A culture that has a high rating on the four elements of authenticity, attachment, pride, and fun is described as having a high emotional capital rating. Companies with higher emotional capital ratings are positively associated with greater profitability, greater revenue growth, and an increased ability to innovate. In contrast, companies with low emotional capital ratings are associated with poor use of technology and an inability to respond to market changes. Leaders in the high-performing corporations are three to four times more likely to frequently make use of corporate collaboration platforms in an effort to extend their influence more broadly across their organizations.

Collaboration platform suppliers often stress the importance of executive participation in collaborative networking programs; however, the nature of that participation is frequently ambiguous. Organizational leaders may want to ask, "How do we succeed in establishing a culture that will support transforming our organization to value customer time?" As a team, executives should undergo training, coaching, and planning to communicate more effectively on internal social networks. Collaboration is a team effort, and the employees will quickly decipher whether their leaders who choose to participate are doing so as an individual or part of a larger cohesive team. More specifically, the team must be trained to focus their communication strategies to accomplish the following:

- Promote authenticity in relationships among employees

- Give employees a sense of pride

- Help employees feel attachment to the communities of shared values and interests

- Inject a sense of fun (in a purposeful way) into the workplace

- Help employees understand the overarching goal of valuing customer time better than the competition

Accomplishing those goals will increase a leadership team's ability to transform the organization to a real-time organization. More specifically, that should encourage people to respond positively to use of the people lever.

Among the most successful companies in this area, executives work as a team and coach one another on their communication efforts. When executives coordinate their communication efforts and allow those relationships to be visible, it serves to inspire all of the employees to work together as a group. Working together, executive teams can discuss overarching goals and communication strategies. They can also coordinate the conversations, messaging, and approaches they take to communicate on internal social networks. In addition, these executives often institute a process that makes use of metrics to measure positive progress and to detect negative reactions that may warrant adjustments.

Example of Joint Use of Core Levers with the People Lever

Core transformational levers may be employed in conjunction with the people lever. Consider an example where, under a new process, a company's customers are able to enter order details directly to the factory floor and check on production status themselves rather than going through a salesperson. Besides freeing salespersons from having to support numerous customer inquiries, which slows their ability to support other customers, it also allows customers direct access to their order information on demand. Such a transformation program can be designed to include a process that analyzes customer-driven change orders in an effort to dynamically identify emerging trends that can systemically alter subcontractor order quantities.

In this example, the process lever is the driving lever that changes the procedure for entering orders and checking production status. That includes use of an important supporting tool within the process lever—information and communications technology—that unlocks the organization's ability to demonstrate that it values customer time. Another lever needed to support these changed processes is the data lever. Properly designed, the data lever collects and drives data and inquiries to the enterprise resource planning (ERP) system, to the trend/market analytics system, to the RTMR system, to management dashboards, and to customer relationship management systems. This example also uses the people lever as a support function to ensure that everyone involved—including customers, salespeople, information systems personnel, and data analysts—all understand the steps in the new processes and how they increase the company's ability to improve interactions with their customers. Furthermore, if the transformational program requires the onboarding of new information and communication technology, the involved personnel need to be trained on the technology before the new processes can be developed or put in place.

Providing Useful Tools for Geographically Distributed Teams—A USC Marshall Research Project

An important aspect of a real-time company is that it is able to respond quickly to customer requests for new products or services. Product development programs can be lengthy, and customers generally accept that delivery of a quality product with immediate turnaround is unreasonable. The need to be real time in a product development setting means that the company is able to respond as fast as or faster than the competition with a similar product at a similar level of quality. A company's ability to respond quickly to such requests is often dependent on its ability to quickly assemble the necessary experts and technology required to satisfy the demand.

In many instances, teams of people must work together to complete each step in the life of a product or service, e.g., designing, producing, or maintaining it. These teams link with each other in complex and evolving ways as the product or service evolves throughout its life. The staff associated with these teams often resides at different geographic locations. Collectively, the personnel involved in such efforts typically include a mix of employees within a company's different locations and affiliated staff employed by partnered companies that are also located at different locations. It is usually logistically unreasonable to bring all the involved parties together in one place, so the organization logically organizes the teams as a series of geographically distributed (or virtual) teams. These distributed teams have the advantage of being created from personnel with valuable and needed skills, even when working in different locations. But this approach also has the disadvantage of geographic separation, which complicates the interaction between team members.

Historically, a geographically distributed team would make heavy use of travel to periodic remote physical meetings to communicate more clearly and maintain team cohesion. Today's information and communication technologies allow members of geographically distributed teams to communicate and function remotely from one another, reducing (though not eliminating) the need for unproductive and costly travel.

Geographically distributed teams often have problems that are rooted in coordination and communication issues. USC Marshall researched these problems in an engineering context to discover that in many cases the communication regimens are often held constant throughout a project's life even though some communication processes work better during design phases and others work better during review phases. A product's life can be divided into a series of design (also known as creation) and corresponding review tasks. For example, these tasks could include the design (or creation) and review of requirements definition, conceptual design, detailed design, development, production, and support. During each review, the design team is responsible for providing an accurate, concise overview of that design task to date so the design can be evaluated and coordinated with other parallel design tasks. Reviewers are responsible for assessing the design to ensure that the current state will properly feed future tasks, allowing the product to be produced, tested, installed, operated, and maintained on schedule and in a manner that is acceptable to customers.[60] The design and review tasks differ and have disparate coordination and communication needs.[61]

The most successful companies accept that design and review processes are fundamentally different and structure their coordination and communication processes around the specific tasks they are intended to support. When geographically distributed teams are reviewing an engineering artifact (the output from a design task), current methods of electronic coordination and communication, such as email, phone, speakerphone, and videoconference, appear to be adequate. In these environments, individual teams are allowed the freedom to select a review methodology that is most comfortable for the individual team members. However, these same methods of electronic coordination and communication are not adequate to support the geographically distributed design of those same artifacts.

Companies possess a variety of tools that can be employed to improve the ability of their people to respond to customer requests for new products or services. Since research has identified different tools as better for different situations, a company selecting a project management tool set should, ideally, select those that are a best fit for the task at hand.

However, the most difficult challenge for the company is not the tool selection process but facilitating the adoption of the tools by the people performing those tasks. Given that each design and review task is different, leaders will be faced with deciding whether to adopt an optimal tool set for each phase despite the incremental adoption costs or whether a suboptimal tool set that avoids unnecessary adoption costs is superior.

Successful companies find many shortfalls with traditional communication methodologies during the design tasks. Many companies simply accept that the use of traditional tools with geographically distributed teams will lower efficiency and slow progress. Because of these shortfalls, many companies use face-to-face meetings to supplement videoconference meetings. Though this may be considered a possible best practice, it is difficult to strike the correct balance between the two options. Face-to-face meetings put a large travel burden on the team, whereas videoconferencing often reduces the effectiveness required between team members when facing complex problems.

Many existing project management tools are targeted for use by well-defined and localized new product development programs. As projects become more complex and involve a larger number of external partners and more geographically distributed teams, new tools are needed to support communication and coordination. Many available tools are not able to deal with complicated ideas that span organizational and geographical boundaries. Specifically, many are not able to perform consensus building and consensus checking.

It is not hard to find examples of development teams that are spread around the world. In these situations, there is no common time zone that allows a review meeting during business hours. Ideally, design and review tasks can be conducted without the inconvenience and expense of asking talented personnel to travel or work late at night or early in the morning. Until the next generation of tools begins to emerge, real-time companies will continue to jockey in an effort to use the existing technology so people can communicate as responsively as possible.

Key Takeaways

- The people lever is one of the core levers for transforming customer real-time experiences. Organizational leaders who decide to use the people lever see a need for employees, customers, suppliers, or relevant others to change. They may also see a need to hire people or work with people beyond current participants to bring about change.

- For people to value customer time better, they must have the motivation and skills to do so. To align people's motivations with valuing customer time, leaders can focus on helping the people involved in a transformation understand what it means to value customer time, why it is important, and how they can help achieve the objective. Training and education programs for employees as well as other important players, including customers and suppliers, are an important component for successful use of the people lever.

- Organizational leaders should recognize that they play a significant role in establishing a positive corporate culture. A question they should ask themselves is, "How do we succeed in establishing a culture that will encourage people to respond positively to use of the people lever?" The answer is found in better communication. As with other employees, leaders will benefit from targeted training and education directed, in this case, at helping them learn to communicate better using contemporary tools.

- Successful use of the people lever includes providing people with tools that provide better support for their actions and interactions. For example, various tools support real-time communication and coordination. However, the need to develop better real-time tools is apparent when people interact to address complex issues with more external partners and geographically distributed teams.

- Organizations that have joined the real-time revolution use the people lever by itself and in conjunction with other core levers to make transformations that value customer time better than competitors. Even when one of the other levers is employed to drive a transformational project, the people lever is likely to be an important complementary lever.

Chapter

8

Going beyond the Core Levers to Transform to a More Real-Time Organization

In 2014, a seven-ton Tyrannosaurus rex skeleton made an incredible journey from Bozeman, Montana, to Washington, DC, in just forty-eight hours. This priceless cargo required special handling, a carefully maintained temperature, and seamless security during transport. The bones were wrapped in custom-made plaster cradles and packed into sixteen foam-filled boxes sealed with special tape. The main crate was equipped with SenseAware, a FedEx innovation that can monitor location, interior temperature, shock, light exposure, and more. This meant the team could respond if, say, the crates got hotter or colder than they should, or if the lid was lifted. The team used a specially equipped eighteen-wheeler with two-way satellite communications, a status-tracking system, emergency alert capabilities, and cargo lock-and-seal services. The T. rex arrived safe and sound, on loan to the Smithsonian National Museum of Natural History.[62]

This example illustrates the use of innovative technologies to support FedEx's quest to become a more real-time organization. As stated by FedEx executive Ed Clarke, "As part of our quest to provide ever better and faster service to our customers, we are now busy investigating today's key technologies in mobility, automation, and sustainability, such as drones, robotics, and platooning."[63]

To continue transforming to a more real-time organization that values customer time better than competitors do, experienced real-time leaders will find that they must go beyond the core levers of products, services, processes, data, and people. Additional levers are particularly important when a company's efforts to become increasingly real time have engaged more and more of the organization or require the cooperation of partners, suppliers, and other affiliated organizations. Such transformational levers include:

- **Technology,** which refers to platforms or more specific tools, machinery, and equipment; more generally, it refers to the means that enable completion of one or more steps at various stages in the life of a product or service. For example, a handsaw is a tool for cutting wood to build a house. Alternative technologies for that same step include a more powerful piece of equipment (viz., an electric handsaw), a more versatile platform (viz., a table saw), and a more automated platform (viz., a numerically controlled milling machine). Technologies do not directly make the company a real-time company but instead can be employed to transform its ability to meet customer needs associated with its products and services. Such was the case with FedEx's use of innovative technologies. Enabling technologies can be deployed within the company or by a partner, such as a supply chain customer.

- **Culture,** which refers to the principles that guide and shape a company's operations. At the core of culture is the set of values shared by the members of the company and, more broadly, the members of its ecosystem of trading partners. Value statements that are posted on the wall or the website reflect management's desired culture, but the company's real culture is often more nuanced and complicated—it may even be the antithesis of management's desired result.

- **Strategy,** which refers to the company's effort to position itself in a changing marketplace. Strategies are often (but not always) documented in a strategic plan that outlines the role the company wants to play in the marketplace. Strategies can be internal to the company or they can include efforts to position the company jointly with other affiliated members of the ecosystem. Strategies should identify long-term goals and distinctive activities that serve to differentiate the company from competitors.

- **Relationships,** which refer to a company's efforts to secure and nurture interactions with its suppliers, customers, and other external parties. In recognizing that their organization, products, and services are part of a larger ecosystem, leaders will increasingly find it beneficial to work with expanding ecosystem partners where each company works to help each other become more real time.

When companies are working within or as part of a complex ecosystem of partners, this working arrangement creates the need for some transformation projects to drive change to entities outside the organization. There are times when a company's efforts to become more real time can be hampered or completely undercut unless a partnered company undertakes a complementary transformational action.

Technology

Technology innovation enables process improvement. As a prerequisite step, it is essential that the enabling technology is deployed and certified for operation before the organization begins to change the selected process. Deployment of the enabling technology in and of itself does not provide any real-time improvement for the company. These improvements only begin to come about after the technology is deployed and the process changes begin. If the process changes fail to bring about the desired result because of an enabling technology fault, the reputation of a desirable transformation program will be harmed. When programs are viewed under a harsh light by customers, employees, and suppliers, it becomes difficult to maintain the support these programs need to thrive.

In the current digital age, information, computing, communication, and connectivity technologies become part of a wide collection of potential enabling technology levers for transformation. Interfaces and ICT (information and communication technology) were previously identified as tools that support process improvement, such as increasing the network speed so critical information can flow quickly through the enterprise. Innovations in these tools may also be considered when focusing on technology innovations. Some of the more specific digital technologies driving changes are social networking, mobile devices, and cloud computing. Other technologies include artificial intelligence (AI), virtual and augmented reality (VR and AR), robotics, big data, and blockchain. Enabling technologies also include Internet of Things (IoT) technologies that take advantage of low-cost network and sensor/actuator systems to permit a myriad of "things" to digitize sensed conditions and respond to remote commands. For example, a smart thermostat and smartphone can be used to control your home temperature from anywhere. These and all other kinds of digital technologies will continue to evolve.

Introducing a new enabling technology has the potential to reduce a company's internal operational time and costs. Some of these enabling technologies can lock a company into new operational processes that are difficult to move away from. The deployment of an enabling technology must be considered from two perspectives: the real-time benefit that the enabling technology supports and risks to future transformational programs associated with the potential for lock-in. Leaders know that the only constant in today's business world is change. No matter how real time a company is today, a competitor is working to find a way to steal the company's real-time crown. As that day approaches, the company must plan to make itself even more responsive if it wants to maintain its leadership position. If an enabling technology precludes that next evolutionary step (a step forward that might not be understood today), the current real-time benefit must be weighed against the cost of that future inhibitor.

Another concern for corporate management is rooted in the negative consequences that enabling technologies, such as automation, can have for employees. Any technology that replaces human workers can have negative consequences for the workforce. Employees are very aware of the potential for technology displacement; they are fearful of these consequences and, therefore, often passively or actively resist such programs. Companies are well advised to consider the negative consequences from adopting an enabling technology. Creating a proactive position on these issues would be wise. The reason that most transformation programs fail is that the corporate culture fails to fully embrace changes required to maximize program success. For example, if management considered the adoption of an automation technology, the leaders must consider how displaced workers will be managed after the program completes. Can they be redeployed or retrained to cover other functions, or should they be given an outplacement package that the employees (both outplaced and those that remain on staff) consider fair? Additionally, in this situation, the leaders must also consider whether the automation technology will lead to a dehumanization of work that could negatively impact employee morale and productivity. If leaders do not co-develop the plan with employees, they should at least share the plan with them to validate or revise it and encourage their needed support.

An example of a pervasive technology-driven change is the adoption, enhancement, and continued expansion of enterprise resource planning (ERP) systems. For companies that make use of ERP systems, changes in these systems are considered advances in an enabling technology, but for companies that sell ERP systems these same changes are considered an advance in their product/services.[64] The advances in a range of global supply chain technologies represent increasingly important enabling technologies for most companies. However, for the logistics companies themselves, they would consider these advances as product and service enhancements. The nature of the transformational lever is often a matter of perspective.

The Future Outlook of Global Supply Chains— A USC Marshall Research Project[65]

An important focus of supply chains is delivering a product from point A to point B in the most efficient manner possible. Managing the physical logistics of goods in transit includes a significant amount of uncertainty. For example, successful delivery of the package may be impacted by issues associated with global strife, transport costs, labor issues, and much more. Companies' ability to remain competitive in an uncertain and changing landscape depends on how well their supply chains are managed. To minimize the risks associated with supply chain issues, most companies seek to establish partnerships with more than one supply chain partner. The existence of multiple supply chain partners also allows the company the freedom to select the delivery service that provides the ideal mix of cost, quality, and time that its customers require. When logistics companies compete against one another as real-time companies, their time-related improvement programs often include efforts to improve supply chain efficiency and agility. For these companies, agility refers to their efforts to adjust schedules to maintain efficiency while reducing delivery times and also improving their ability to react and recover from unexpected situations.

The critical nature of supply chain management has continued to balloon with globalization, and these same globalization processes are continuing to spread. By 2025 the world's consuming class is expected to grow to 4.2 billion people, and all of these people will be able to order products online and have them delivered by a sophisticated and networked supply chain. By 2030 the world's 750 biggest cities will contribute over 60 percent of the total world GDP, and these cities will act as natural hubs required to support the supply chain ecosystem.[66]

Supply chains are not static networks but grow, expand, and evolve over time; their ability to do so is dramatically impacted by advancements in enabling technologies employed by this industry. Some of these new technologies allow goods to move faster through the supply chain, others allow goods to be better tracked, and others allow the business processes that support these endeavors to operate more efficiently. The disruptive impact of these enabling technologies is continuing to change how companies manage their supply chains, and often the early adopters are able to leverage these technologies for a competitive advantage.

The USC Marshall research found that the majority of companies do not have a team in charge of their supply chain. Of the companies that do have such a team, the majority have a global presence. The research also found that the fastest-growing companies in today's market are global companies. As logistics companies continue to improve their international services, the expectation is that even these successful global companies will move away from centralized supply chain structures.

A majority of successful companies indicate they are increasing their focus on e-commerce preparedness projects, allowing them to directly fulfill and ship orders placed on the internet (hands-free). Cloud technologies have already had a significant impact on supply chain and other business practices. For some companies, though, these and other enabling supply chain technologies represent a new step forward, complete with risks and costs. However, there are also situations where companies have experience with an enabling technology and are considering its use in a new way to support supply chain processes. In a transformation program involving the adoption of a new supply chain technology or the extension of already adopted technology, the information technology (IT) group is often a key contributor. Thus, it is important that IT specialists, supply chain specialists, and other transformation team members collaborate with each other throughout adoption and implementation of the technology. Companies that have had previous success working collaboratively on innovation projects will find it easier to bring the team together early in the project's life so the collaborative benefits begin right away. Other companies may need to make special efforts to nurture collaboration.

Though logistics companies continually compete to become more real time, there are limits associated with the movement of a physical shipment. Efforts to improve the information flow between these service companies and their customers represent attempts to improve customers' experiences as they anticipate receiving or sending a shipment. Thus, the real-time battleground in the supply chain is not only in providing more effective real-time physical shipment of the product but also in the way these logistics companies work with customers to adopt and use e-commerce, cloud, and other emerging technologies to exchange information. Ultimately, these supply chain technologies bring the data lever into play to make better real-time customer experiences possible.

The importance of data should, nevertheless, not obscure other aspects of logistics that improve real-time customer experiences. The importance of packaging is an example:

Frustration-Free Packaging[67]

Hasbro is working with Amazon to reinvent the boxes that hold its games and toys to reduce waste and simplify packaging. "Amazon is great from a collaboration perspective because they help us understand that the shopping journey is changing," said Hasbro's Jeff Jackson.

Hasbro has designed a new Baby Alive box for Amazon's Frustration-Free Packaging program. Frustration-Free Packaging is Amazon's way of cutting down on waste, helping the environment, and reducing what some call "wrap rage"—which comes from the difficulty people occasionally have opening traditional packages with plastic clamshells and wire ties. And it's great for the environment because products are designed and certified to ship in their original packaging, eliminating the need for an additional shipping box. Instead of boxes with large plastic windows to show off a toy, the new packaging Hasbro has designed with Amazon is right-sized and 100 percent recyclable. The packages are also designed to take less than two minutes for a customer to open. Recognizing the importance of the customer's time—even for something as basic as opening a package—is a hallmark of a real-time organization.

Culture

At the core of a company's culture are the values shared by its members. Members of an organization who have previously undertaken a real-time transformation project have learned to place a high value on customer time. Presumably, through this project the team members have also developed an appreciation for the competitive nature of a real-time market environment and how this drives a need for continual innovation. These team members can serve as the company's internal real-time ambassadors. In an ideal world, at the conclusion of one transformational project, the members from that team would be distributed to different transformational programs within the company. These experienced program leaders would help successfully complete other programs while instilling in the other project members a belief in the need for real-time cultural change. Over time, these shared values would become more widely shared, and a real-time culture would naturally emerge. Beyond the organization, if the company forms a transformational team that includes employees from partner companies as members, those same values could be transmitted to allied companies (as long the management of the allied companies are willing to embrace the same philosophies).

As stated by the respected organizational psychologist Edgar Schein,

> *For any given group or organization that has had a substantial history, culture is the pattern of basic assumptions that the group has invented, discovered or developed in learning to cope with its problems of external adaptation and internal integration, and that has worked well enough to be considered valid, and, therefore, to be taught to new members as the correct way to perceive, think, and feel in relation to these problems.*[68]

Changing an organization's culture is a slow process at first, but it can have a compounding effect if the successes that arise from such efforts are celebrated within the company. Success, in this sense, is defined as the visible demonstration that the organization is able to facilitate a customer's real-time experience in a way that is better than similar experiences facilitated by competitors. These successes will not become apparent until after the transformational program is complete and presumably the transformational team has been disbanded. This makes it critical that these operational successes are linked to the transformational team that enabled such successes.

A complex transformational change requires considerable attention both during the implementation and afterward, once the changes become operational. Research has demonstrated that the major reasons for the failure of such efforts are often associated with insufficient commitment on the part of management in terms of time and/or resources. Often these programs are under-scoped; they take time to mature, and the time required to realize results is often underestimated. Finally, companies often neglect to provide an adequate socialization program or create a sufficient training and development program for the personnel involved. These programs can include memos/directives from top management, formal training programs, discussion groups among impacted employees, circulation of success stories, and incentive programs that encourage the evolving cultural values. Leaders will be particularly watched for their determination to follow through on new goals. They must be ready with progress metrics that allow for assessment of the success of their efforts.[69]

Strategy

Strategy is reflected in the distinctive activities a company employs to differentiate it from competitors and achieve its goals. Within a real-time company's strategy, there are distinctive activities that can be associated with the company's desire to become a real-time organization. Creating a high-quality customer experience is a differentiation strategy; the focus on the customer's time as a critical component of the customer experience is a defining characteristic of the real-time company.[70] Thus, the real-time organization's activities to demonstrate a respect and a sense of value for the customer's time often differentiate it from the competition.

Companies should establish a transformational roll-out plan. The success (or lack of success) of the initial projects sets the tone for future real-time-inspired transformations. Often an organization's first real-time transformational program is limited; the organization's ability to evolve is constrained by its ability to appreciate the need for a company to change. As a result, these earliest efforts are often separated from the rest of the organization. A segmented structure may force the transformational team to struggle once the program begins to be integrated into the company, but it avoids complications early in the program's life that are associated with mixing two distinct corporate cultures. After a number of successful real-time transformations have been completed, the focus on the customer will be accepted as a paramount concern. Over time, the successful organization will find itself involved in running several concurrent transformational programs. Ideally, the elements involved in the changes will no longer need to be segmented from the rest of the organization because the process will seem second nature to the company.

For some companies, demonstrating the value of customer time more effectively than the competition becomes integral to the organization's strategy. In other words, organizations that base their strategy on valuing customer time are following a real-time organizational strategy that, while rooted in the original corporate strategy, ultimately redefines the company's core product or service value proposition.

Relationships with Suppliers, Customers, and Other Partners

Suppliers, customers, and other partners that interact with an organization all have a relationship with the organization. Using the core levers to transform the organization to value customer time more effectively than the competition may lead to changing relationships with these stakeholders. These relationships are important levers to consider as potential drivers to improve the company's real-time position in the market.

Digital technologies make it possible for organizations to reimagine their relationships with customers to be more than a transactional interaction. Loyalty programs with retailers are examples of one type of relationship that digital technology makes possible. These programs involve unobtrusively collecting data on items purchased by customers. Analysis of these purchases allows retailers to understand customers' purchasing behaviors and preferences. That understanding permits retailers to more effectively tailor information, products, and services to satisfy these customers and their preferences, ideally providing more effective real-time experiences. Customers are often more than happy to share data with a company they trust as long as that information is utilized to provide them with a better customer experience. However, customers become concerned when that data is not protected or is shared with outside parties, which the customer might not trust.

Sensor technology is increasingly being employed to collect data on a product's use over its life. This data can be generated by monitoring a product's performance or reporting that data to a service organization so the company can provide timely preventive maintenance. Such preemptive service saves the customer time, particularly if the customer believes the product fills an essential need. This is an example of how technology is utilized to change the relationship between the company and the customer.

ServiceMax[71]

The field service industry is huge, encompassing twenty million field technicians in vans spread across the world, maintaining everything from hospital equipment to office elevators, heavy manufacturing machines, and wind farm turbines. Reductions in the time it takes to address problems can have huge consequences. IoT technology—sensors and real-time monitoring—can identify problems or potential problems that should be addressed so that service technicians with the right skills, repair parts, and tools can be rapidly and efficiently dispatched to serve customers in need.

ServiceMax is a leading participant in the field service management (FSM) market. Through its IoT-driven cloud service management platform, marketed as Connected Field Service (CFS), customers can use "predictive maintenance," i.e., fix problems before they occur. Medical equipment manufacturer Medivators has implemented CFS across its international operations. The company has seen a 78 percent increase in the number of service events that can be diagnosed and corrected remotely, with no need to dispatch a field technician. Using the relationships and technology levers to address field service problems remotely has made Medivators and ServiceMax more real-time organizations than when service problems were addressed by dispatching a field technician.

Some relationships may involve a different kind of problem known as a chicken-and-egg problem. In these relationships, a company's partners are independent organizations that have no direct reporting relationship to the company but are needed to satisfy the customer's product or service requirements. Incentivizing a partner to act in support of a company's efforts to make itself a real-time company is a matter of negotiation. However, despite the existence of a negotiated agreement, the company cannot ensure the partner will successfully serve the company's interests. Many times a company will take action to improve the probability of success for its partners. Without such an intervention, the partner could fail, which precludes the company from achieving its objectives. This class of problems is sometimes characterized as chicken-and-egg problems, i.e., problems where the company must act to ensure another company's success before it can be successful.

A Chicken-and-Egg Situation for Fuel Cell Electric Vehicles and Filling Stations

Many innovative transformational programs face one or more chicken-and-egg issues. For example, consider the situation where electric car manufacturers need charging stations before they can sell their vehicles, and the providers of the charging stations require a sufficient number of electric cars before they can be successful. Without a sufficient quantity of electric cars, few, if any, charging stations will be established; without sufficient charging stations, few, if any, electric cars will be demanded. Trying to secure cooperation between independent companies (e.g., to have enough charging stations and electric cars for each to succeed) renders these chicken-and-egg problems difficult to solve.[72]

True Zero

The report A California Road Map, published in 2012, represents a collaborative and collective effort by various stakeholders to design a pragmatic road map for hydrogen station placement, enabling the deployment of tens of thousands of fuel cell electric vehicles (FCEVs) in California. This effort reflects input and consensus from more than thirty partners, including auto manufacturers, energy companies, fuel cell technology companies, government agencies, nongovernmental organizations, and universities. Incentive funding is widely acknowledged as necessary to make the business case for investing in these early commercial stations. Early stations are not expected to be fully utilized, and therefore not profitable, during the initial commercialization years. Early market consumers must be confident that sufficient fueling is available, whether near their home, work, or desirable destinations.

True Zero of Irvine, California, is the consumer-facing brand of hydrogen filling stations owned by FirstElement Fuel. It is at the center of an effort by automakers and regulators to develop the infrastructure to support the growing number of fuel cell vehicles on the market. FirstElement announced plans to build nineteen stations in California in 2015. Honda and Toyota provided $13.8 million in loans to spur construction of True Zero stations. FirstElement also received $27.6 million in grants from the California Energy Commission and another $2 million in grants from regional air-quality management districts.

The True Zero stations are installed in existing filling stations. This is more economical than developing sites from scratch, easier from a permitting perspective, and more amenable to new hydrogen customers. Automakers such as Honda and Toyota are keen to do what they can to ease their customers' experience with hydrogen—just as Tesla did with its network of Supercharger stations.

Some potential negative consequences of the chicken-and-egg problem include:

- Failure of promising innovations, which includes discontinuation of projects due to insufficient cash flow or other difficulties

- Disincentive to bring out promising innovations, which include situations where a promising innovative idea might disrupt established and solid cash flows associated with legacy businesses

- Failure to reach critical mass, which includes situations where there are delays getting to the crossover point that allows the businesses to become self-sustaining

With these types of chicken-and-egg problems, one company could execute its strategy flawlessly, but if the other company fails to successfully execute its strategy, the market will work to ensure that both companies suffer negative consequences.

Over time, as ecosystems continue to become more complex, some companies that are working together on a chicken-and-egg issue may evolve their relationship. Such an evolving relationship anticipates merger and acquisition, a licensing arrangement, or the formation of a more formal strategic alliance. Other companies may not evolve their relationship but instead may allow it to linger or languish. Although the potential for success in such situations is often clouded, as long as there is the possibility of success, these relations will persist. Despite their complexity, a network of ecosystem partners has the potential to outperform a single vertically integrated company. As a company's partnerships proliferate and as market problems/solutions become more complex, the number of chicken-and-egg issues and proposed solutions will increase. Just as relationships with suppliers, customers, and others are important levers to consider as potential drivers to improve a company's real-time position in the market, so are relationships with partners in a chicken-and-egg situation.

Addressing Chicken-and-Egg Problems with Ecosystem Partners—A USC Marshall Research Project

Although chicken-and-egg issues are relatively common, work on the chicken-and-egg issue in managing innovations has been relatively scarce. USC Marshall research[73] demonstrates there is substantial agreement with the following statements:

- When evaluating the potential of new products and services that a company may offer, chicken-and-egg problems are often a significant issue.

- Chicken-and-egg problems often make new innovations more difficult to pursue.

- Unanticipated chicken-and-egg problems can emerge as an unexpected source of friction once a development project begins to make progress.

This research also found that business leaders felt that their companies' ability to address chicken-and-egg problems gave them a significant competitive advantage.

Two broad classes of problems arise when forming an alliance as a strategic response to addressing the chicken-and-egg problem. One class of problems arises from responding to unanticipated events, such as external events or unexpected actions from the partner. Sources of external events include technological changes and competitor actions; sources of unexpected partner actions include different cultures, conflicting goals, and different decision-making styles. The danger is that these unanticipated events lead to divergent incentives or debilitating conflicts.

The second class of problems is based on concerns of being taken advantage of by the partner. In this situation, one or both companies assume the cooperative arrangement creates a relationship of unequal partners (i.e., an unbalanced relationship) where one company begins taking actions to inoculate itself from the actions of the other. An example of this class of problem would include making specific investments that benefit one partner but fail to lead to appropriate benefits for the other partner. Another example occurs when a company is losing its technology edge or other proprietary information, thereby nullifying the cooperative spirit that allows both entities to flourish. Withholding key information from a trusted partner negatively impacts the partner's performance, and in chicken-and-egg situations, this reduction in performance actually harms both companies. Thus, it is essential that a company share its intellectual property when appropriate, but in a way that still provides adequate protection.

Ultimately, trust becomes an important determinant of the positive resolution of these chicken-and-egg issues. Among firms that rely on third parties to source or implement new technologies, there is a strong preference to work with vendors with whom they have developed a trusted working relationship. For companies where this is not possible, the companies find they must evolve and develop a trusted relationship before progress accelerates.

Companies must consider three major types of alliances—contractual alliance, joint venture, and merger or acquisition—when they decide to become formally involved in a chicken-and-egg relationship. These three options fall on a continuum from the least integrated to completely integrated. The assumption is that companies in a chicken-and-egg relationship recognize that they must develop something more than an arm's-length relationship, i.e., something more than a customer-supplier relationship.

A key ingredient in any form of alliance is based on the expectations associated with the alliance. Firms need to understand the importance of setting and managing expectations from both sides. Many problems in contractual alliances, joint ventures, and acquisitions are related to misaligned expectations. If firms do not take the time to carefully manage expectations, then different groups often draw from their different backgrounds to create differing expectations. When expectations are not met, that triggers frustration, anger, and distrust. Therefore, it is imperative to clearly align expectations.

The contract for a contractual alliance or joint venture is different from a contract for a merger or acquisition; however, the negotiation process provides a similar context for the setting of expectations. Clear communication is essential for all forms of alliance.

Trust is also essential for a successful partnership, and there must be a fully disclosed win-win game plan. If both companies are on an equitable win-win game plan, then when one company is experiencing difficulty, the other company should step in to aid in their mutual success. Mutual trust implies that one company will freely admit to the other if there is a problem. If either company attempts to obfuscate a problem, that reflects a misalignment in values. Moreover, beyond sharing what each side expects of the other, a successful alliance results in each company disclosing to the other any incidents of program failure. If one company's actions are inconsequential to the other, the other company is unlikely to do anything to support the former when there is trouble.

For a real-time organization to work successfully with partners in a chicken-and-egg alliance, all partners must put a high priority on valuing customer time. That priority clearly needs to be a common expectation. The partners should discuss in detail what that priority means for the alliance.

Key Takeaways

- To transform their organizations to value customer time more effectively than competitors, leaders may find that they must go beyond the core levers of:
  - ▸ Product or service innovations
  - ▸ Process innovations
  - ▸ Innovations with data
  - ▸ Innovations through people
- Changes involving these broader levers include innovations in:
  - ▸ Technology
  - ▸ Culture
  - ▸ Strategy
  - ▸ Relationships with suppliers, customers, and others in the organization's ecosystem
- Organizational leaders should ask themselves, "What levers are we ready to use?"
  - ▸ Organizations that have joined the real-time revolution with aspirations to be real-time leaders will find themselves employing these broader levers.
  - ▸ Organizations that have tried a limited set of transformation projects to become more real time using the core levers may find that they are ready to try a transformation project with a broader lever.
  - ▸ Organizations that are not ready to consider these broader levers should at least try using one or more of the core levers to become a more real-time organization.
  - ▸ Organizations failing to use any of these levers are missing the real-time revolution and threatening their survival.

Conclusion

Take the Next and Continuing Steps of the Real-Time Revolution

Google Maps has a user interface that is intuitive, routes that are easy to set up, and navigational guidance that is simple to follow.[74] Google has taken a huge amount of off-line information, compiled the data, and published the resulting view online. That includes highway networks, road signs, street names, and business names. To aid this endeavor, Google has established its Base Map Partner Program. Many governmental, commercial, educational, and nonprofit agencies submit detailed vector data to Google. These agencies include the US Forest Service, the US National Park Service, the US Geological Survey, and various city and county councils. This data, which periodically changes, helps keep the "base map" as up to date as possible.

The amount of data constantly being reviewed by Google includes data from its Street View program, satellite imagery data from Google Earth, and individual enthusiast data from its Local Guides program. This information is then integrated with Google's business listings to provide an even more complete view of the neighborhood. Sophisticated algorithms link this data together, spot inconsistencies, and make the data easy to access.

Google is constantly updating its mapping data to ensure that customers have an accurate and up-to-date view of their environment. When Google updates Google Maps, it is applying the product lever to ensure that mapping data is an accurate reflection of the customer's surroundings. Google's customers depend on Google Maps to route them to their destinations quickly.[75] By making its customers more efficient, Google is demonstrating that it recognizes the importance of time for its customers. The competing services to Google Maps understand the importance of accurate information that drives competing routing algorithms. The navigation space is a sector where a company's ability to provide accurate real-time services is the driving differentiator.

Time is a scarce resource that customers cannot replace once it is spent. Therefore, customers are motivated to spend their time wisely. They are drawn to products or services from organizations that best allow them to meet this need. This need will only increase as more is expected of individuals in their already busy days. With speed as the measure of effectiveness for many products or services, the product that is the fastest will have a competitive advantage. The product's ease of use demands less training time. The product that has high quality requires less product support. The product that is easy to discover, order, and receive makes the customer even more efficient. Companies that do not live up to the competitive pressure on these fronts will be forced to discount their offerings to offset the advantage of the competitors. And, as time becomes even more valuable, these discounts must be increased.

Best-in-class products and services set the customer's real-time standard. As new products appear in the market, they are immediately compared with a wide range of direct and indirect offerings in an effort to determine whether the new product makes the customer more effective. Organizations whose products demonstrate that the company values customer time by meeting or beating an established real-time standard will have a significant competitive advantage.

Customers' real-time experiences go beyond their use of a company's products and services. Their experiences include every interaction with the company, throughout all steps in the life of those products and services. As potential customers are browsing a company's website, they begin to develop an opinion of the company. When they read content published on the internet, they consider whether they would like to work with the company. When customers decide to purchase a product and initiate the ordering process, they are looking for an experience that is relevant, efficient, and clear. When customers upgrade the product or seek answers to support questions, they are deciding whether this is a company they wish to continue to support. Just as customers desire to optimize the time spent using many products and services, they also want their other interactions with the company to demonstrate an equal level of attention to the value of their time. In the ideal real-time experience, customers want interactions that are instantaneously effective. A real-time organization aspires to provide ideal real-time experiences, knowing that it may not succeed. If it can beat its competitors, though, it will set the standard for customer real-time experiences and have a clear competitive advantage.

Customers develop their time expectations from the experiences they have with other organizations, both direct and indirect competitors. For example, if a customer finds an online retailer to have a particularly useful and efficient browsing and ordering process, that customer will expect other online companies to be equally efficient. This does not mean the online travel site must mirror the online retailer, but it should strive to be as customer efficient. If a competing online travel store launches with a more streamlined user interface that equals the online retailer's efficiency, it stands to gain significant market share over time. Those organizations that meet or beat customers' real-time expectations will attract more customers.

Quality is a key component to understanding customers' time value. Customers want their experiences to be of sufficient quality that they do not need to spend their personal time overcoming a problematic product or interacting with the company to solve a problem. For example, customers expect the maps in a navigation application to be accurate or they could be sent to the wrong destination and then forced to find an alternate route.

For some products and services, customers desire experiences that focus more on the quality of time spent rather than the duration. For example, pleasurable dining and entertainment experiences are often designed to be savored. For these types of experiences, the customers expect the company to maximize their enjoyment over time. However, when the customer is seeking a quick dining or entertainment experience, they have different expectations that are constrained by time. A fast-food restaurant experience is very different from a fine dining experience. Similarly, a full-length feature film is different from a television program, and the experience is again different for a short video that one might watch while standing in line at the DMV.

Customers develop relationships with the companies they patronize. A company wants the journey a customer takes with it to be a long and mutually beneficial relationship. Within the journey, the time the customer spends with the company can be broken into segments. Organizations that meet better time expectations associated with a specific time segment are often positively remembered. These experiences, such as the time to make reservations, make payments, and travel to and from the experiences, provide the company with a competitive advantage as long as the quality of the time spent meets or beats expectations. When these time segments are assembled together, only then does the totality of the journey become visible. If a company fails to meet the customer's expectation in one segment of the journey, the deficit can be offset by exceeding the customer's expectations during other aspects of the journey. However, it is important to understand that the priority customers place on specific time segments may vary by industry, segment, and customer.

Given that time is the currency that customers spend wisely, the implication for organizational leaders is that they must transform their organizations to value customer time more effectively than competitors do. Those leaders who do not do so are in danger of losing customers to organizations that provide experiences that meet or beat customer real-time expectations.

Leaders of organizations that join the real-time revolution constantly monitor how effective their company is at valuing customer time compared to the competition. To accomplish this, the company establishes a monitoring process to track where customers spend time. For example, before and during the ordering process, the time a customer spends on the company's website is tracked. Products use IoT-sourced data to self-detect product issues and time until there is a correction. When customers call for support, time is tracked from initial contact and, perhaps, other checkpoints until the customer confirms resolution of the issue. Requests for new products as well as product enhancements are tracked from the time the request is made until the request is satisfied.

All these time measurements are tracked in an RTMR (real-time monitoring and response) system. This repository allows a company to analyze its ability to respond and support customer interactions. This analysis permits the company to target transformational innovations to specific projects that increase customer appreciation. Customers appreciate companies that respect them, and since time is increasingly the most precious resource a customer has, this translates to efforts that improve the customer's effective use of time.

In a competitive world where the competition always seeks to displace the market leader, a real-time market leader must constantly improve its ability to perform. Companies that are not the market leader know that they and the market leader are in a perpetual race to better themselves. This means that the non-leader companies that want to remain competitive must target their efforts to surpass the market leader. Identifying and matching the known best practice is not enough. Companies must pursue a path that positions them to become the new market leader.

Organizations that are participating in the real-time revolution are in a constant cycle of transforming; they innovate, monitor, analyze, and then innovate some more. The perpetual goal is to demonstrate a more refined and effective means of valuing customer time more than the competition.

To survive and thrive in the real-time revolution, organizational leaders must transform their organizations to value customer time more effectively than competitors do.

- The real-time organization must engage customers from end to end, i.e., throughout the steps in the life of its products and services. The purpose is to have customers view the organization as valuing their time and, thus, meeting their real-time expectations better than competitors do.

- The real-time organization must be agile enough to detect and respond to changing customer real-time expectations more rapidly than competitors.

- The core organizational levers for transformation are products and services, processes, data, and people driven by a focus on valuing customer time.

- Beyond the core levers are broader levers for transformation, including technology, culture, strategy, and relationships with suppliers, customers, and other partners.

Organizational leaders should ask, "What are my next and continuing steps?" Those who are inspired by this book's message should develop a plan to transform their organizations to value customer time more effectively than competitors do. A road map for the next and continuing steps in the real-time revolution is to follow these incremental steps:

- Ensure that a core set of leaders and other organizational members appreciate the need for the company to become a real-time company; ensure they understand that success in a real-time environment is based on the customer's perception of time.

- Work with these leaders and members to create an RTMR system. Collect monitoring data to identify when and how customers invest and value their time with your organization and the competition.

- Work with leaders and members to begin and follow through on the following steps in a transformational cycle:

  - Analyze the collected data to identify levers that can drive improvement. Focus on areas where the organization can apply one or more levers to maximize the real-time benefit for the customer.

  - Specify the innovation to be implemented using the high-potential levers.

  - Implement that innovation. Be prepared to use additional levers as the need becomes apparent. For example, deploy/acquire any needed prerequisite enabling technologies to apply the high-potential levers.

  - Initiate any needed training or evangelization programs.

  - Expand the RTMR system to monitor the new customer real-time experience data. Innovations often create opportunities to collect incremental process usage data from customers.

  - Collect, update, and analyze the monitoring data in the RTMR system to ensure the transformation improves the end-to-end customer experience.

  - Adjust the transformational process as needed.

- Begin the next transformational cycle.

The first cycle set forth above will take time; companies must develop an appreciation for the fact that using their own internal view of time is not a measure of customer value. Over time, this perspective will become second nature, a matter of the company's culture. Over time, real-time transformational programs can be expanded and multiple programs can be simultaneously run.

For a company, cultural changes are difficult. Whenever possible:

- Work with the transformational program leaders to broadcast to a larger group of employees the need to transform the company to a real-time organization. Build in them an understanding and acceptance of this need so that these employees become the company's real-time warriors.

- Adopt an end-to-end view of the time investment customers make with the company. Empower the organization's real-time warriors by being transparent and sharing information about customers' interactions with the organization.

  - Share customer time consumption associated with your company and the competition.

  - Provide stories of success to demonstrate how customer time value can be increased.

  - Assess customers' real-time experiences with your company and how that compares with the competition.

- Encourage innovation that makes the company more of a real-time company.

Time is a scarce currency for companies and their customers. Customers wish to spend their time wisely, and this drives their appreciation for the real-time company. Companies also must treat their time as a scarce resource. The intent of the RTMR system data is to ensure that a company targets its transformational programs to create a difference that customers appreciate.

Targeted innovations focus on valuing customers' time by providing them with experiences that meet or beat their real-time expectations. These targeted transformations are what give a company a competitive advantage. In the real-time revolution, where competitors are continually innovating to have customers spend time with them, the purpose of continually transforming to a more competitive real-time organization is to survive and thrive. We wish you well in taking the next and continuing steps of the real-time revolution!

Notes

Introduction

1. Travis M. Hessman, "Have It Your Way: Manufacturing in the Age of Mass Customization," *Industry Week*, June 3, 2014. Accessed June 13, 2018 at http://www.industryweek.com/technology/have-it-your-way-manufacturing -age-mass-customization.

2. https://www.dictionary.com/browse/real-time. Accessed 10/28/2018.

3. Omar El Sawy and Pernille Rydén, "The Shades of Grey in Real-Time Management—a Multi-Method Study" (presented to the Institute for Communication Technology Management, Marshall School of Business, University of Southern California, April 29, 2016, available at https://www .marshall.usc.edu/sites/default/files/2019-01/Real-Time %20Management -El%20Sawy%20R3.pdf). There is also an article based on the study: Pernille Rydén and Omar El Sawy, "How Managers Perceive Real-Time Management: Thinking Fast & Flow," *California Management Review* 61, no. 2 (February 2019): 155–177. Article first published online December 19, 2018, https://journals.sagepub.com/doi/abs/10.1177/ 0008125618818840.

4. Peter Forbes, "How Payment Technologies Ease the Pain of Restaurant Bills," Food Newsfeed, *FSR Magazine*, May 2017. Accessed June 12, 2018 at https:// www.foodnewsfeed.com/fsr/vendor-bylines/how-payment-technologies -ease-pain-restaurant-bills.

5. "When Corporate Innovation Goes Bad—The 132 Biggest Product Failures of All Time," CB Insights, June 25, 2018. Accessed August 2, 2018 at https:// www.cbinsights.com/research/corporate-innovation-product-fails; Steve Kovach, "How Samsung Out-Designed Apple," Business Insider, August 2, 2016. Accessed August 2, 2018 at https://www .businessinsider.com/samsung -galaxy-note-7-vs-apple-iphone-design-features-2016-8; Steve Kovach, "Samsung Announces What Caused the Galaxy Note 7 to Overheat and Explode," Business Insider, January 22, 2017. Accessed August 2, 2018 at https://www.businessinsider.com/samsung-issues-galaxy-note-7-battery -report-2017-1; Steve Kovach, "Samsung's Galaxy Note 7 Explanation Didn't Go Far Enough," Business Insider, January 23, 2017. Accessed August 2, 2018 at https:// www.businessinsider.com/samsung-galaxy-note-7-report -what-was-missing-2017-1.

Chapter 1

6. Salesforce Research, *State of the Connected Customer*, 2nd ed., 2018. Accessed December 24, 2018 at https://www.salesforce.com/content/dam/web/en_us/www/documents/e-books/state-of-the-connected-customer-report-second-edition2018.pdf; Salesforce Research, *State of the Connected Customer*, 2016. Accessed December 24, 2018 at https://a.sfdcstatic.com/content/dam/www/ocms/assets/pdf/service-cloud/state-of-connected-customer.pdf.

7. Stop & Shop, "Press Release: Stop & Shop Invests $70 Million in Greater Hartford Stores to Offer New Features Like More Fresh & Healthy Foods, Improved Digital Solutions & Lower Prices on Thousands of Items," October 24, 2018. Accessed December 25, 2018 at https://stopandshop.com/news-and-media/article-10-04-18.

8. Chad Wright, "Customer Care Strategy: Value Your Customer's Time," *MicroAutomation* (blog), August 19, 2018. Accessed December 26, 2018 at https://www.microautomation.com/new-blog/customer-care-strategy-value-your-customers-time.

9. Jeff Toister, "How Fast Should a Business Respond to an Email?" *Inside Customer Service* (Toister Performance Solutions blog), April 17, 2018. Accessed December 24, 2018 at https://www.toistersolutions.com/blog/2018/4/15/how-fast-should-a-business-respond-to-an-email; Jeff Toister, "How Quickly Should You Respond to an Email?" *Inside Customer Service* (blog), Toister Performance Solutions, May 21, 2012. Accessed December 24, 2018 at https://jeff-toister-bvag.squarespace.com/blog/2012/5/21/how-quickly-should-you-respond-to-an-email.html.

10. John DeVine and Keith Gilson, "Applied Insight," *McKinsey Quarterly*, no. 2 (2010): 100–105.

11. El Sawy and Pernille Rydén, "The Shades of Grey in Real-Time Management"; Pernille Rydén and El Sawy, "How Managers Perceive Real-Time Management."

Chapter 2

12. "#1807 Sysmex," Forbes, 2018. Accessed December 29, 2018 at https://www.forbes.com/companies/sysmex/#6f29955047d9.

13. Michael E. Porter and James E. Heppelmann, "How Smart, Connected Products Are Transforming Companies," *Harvard Business Review* 93, no. 10 (October 2015): 96–114. Accessed June 13, 2018 at https://hbr.org/2015/10/how-smart-connected-products-are-transforming-companies; Sysmex, *Sysmex Report 2018*, Sysmex Corporation, 2018. Accessed December 30, 2018 at https://www.sysmex.co.jp/en/ir/library/annual-reports/Sysmex_Report_2018_e.pdf.

14. "Share Your Activity with Your Apple Watch," Apple, 2018. Accessed August 18, 2018 at https://support.apple.com/en-us/HT207014.

15. Oliver Behr, *Fashion 4.0—Digitalization of Fashion*, January 5, 2018. Accessed August 18, 2018 at https://iot.cassini.de/fileadmin/whitepaper /Fashion-4.0_english.pdf.

16. "3 Year Degree Plan," Ohio Department of Higher Education, c. 2012. Accessed August 20, 2018 at https://www.ohiohighered.org/content/3 _year_degree; Sue Shellenbarger, "Universities With Three-Year Bachelor's Degree Programs," *Wall Street Journal*, May 26, 2010. Accessed August 20, 2018 at https://www.wsj.com/articles/SB1000142405274870334190457526663 52925815936; Subhash Kak, "Will Traditional Colleges and Universities Become Obsolete?" Smithsonian.com, January 10, 2018. Accessed August 20, 2018 at https://www.smithsonianmag.com/innovation/will -traditional-colleges-universities-become-obsolete-180967788.

17. Bucher + Suter AG, *b+s Case Study: Republic Services with b+s Connects for Salesforce*, c. 2018. Accessed August 21, 2018 at https://www.bucher-suter .com/crmconnectors/salesforce-integration/download-case-study.pdf.

18. Ibid.

19. For example, here are a few different writings: Rosabeth Moss Kanter, "Innovation: The Classic Traps," *Harvard Business Review* 84, no. 11 (2006): 72–83; Everett M. Rogers, *Diffusion of Innovations*, 5th ed. (New York: The Free Press, 2003); Jane M. Howell and Christopher A. Higgins, "Champions of Technological Innovation," *Administrative Science Quarterly* 35 (1990): 317–341.

Chapter 3

20. Nancy Gondo, "Michael Dell Built a PC Powerhouse via Build-to-Order Model," *Investors Business Daily*, April 15, 2014, A04; Young K. Ro, Jeffrey K. Liker, and Sebastian K. Fixson, "Modularity as a Strategy for Supply Chain Coordination: The Case of U.S. Auto," *IEEE Transactions on Engineering Management* 54, no. 1 (2007): 172–189.

21. Mark Esposito, Terence Tse, and Khaled Soufani, "Companies Are Working with Consumers to Reduce Waste," *Harvard Business Review* (digital articles), June 7, 2016, pp. 2–5. Accessed June 13, 2018 at https://hbr.org /2016/06/companies-are-working-with-consumers-to-reduce-waste; "Sustainability," Nudie Jeans, 2018. Accessed August 26, 2018 at https://www .nudiejeans.com/blog/category/sustainability; "Nudie Jeans Launches Re-Use Online," Nudie Jeans, 2018. Accessed August 26, 2018 at https://cdn .nudiejeans.com/media/files/Press-Release-Re-use.pdf; "Nudie Jeans Repair Tour," Nudie Jeans, June 15, 2018. Accessed August 27, 2018 at https://www .nudiejeans.com/blog/nudie-jeans-mobile-repair-station-on-tour.

22. Jacob Siegal, "Here's How Fast You Can Charge an iPhone 8 Plus with a Variety of Different Chargers," BGR, October 10, 2017. Accessed August 27, 2018 at https://bgr.com/2017/10/10/iphone-8-charging-speeds-fast-charging -iphone-x; "Fast Charge Your iPhone X, iPhone 8, or iPhone 8 Plus," Apple,

June 13, 2018. Accessed August 27, 2018 at https://support .apple.com /en-us/HT208137.

23. "Dyson Supersonic™ Hair Dryer," Dyson, 2018. Accessed August 27, 2018 at https://www.dyson.com/hair-care/dyson-supersonic-overview.html.

24. Kelsey Mulvey, "11 Things That Help Us Get Ready in the Morning Faster," Insider Picks, Business Insider, July 17, 2017. Accessed August 27, 2018 at https://www.businessinsider.com/how-to-get-ready-faster-in-the-morning -2017-5#a-powerful-hair-dryer-4.

25. Cynthia Drescher, "The 10 Fastest Trains in the World," *Condé Nast Traveler*, March 27, 2018. Accessed August 27, 2018 at https://www .cntraveler.com /stories/2016-05-18/the-10-fastest-trains-in-the-world.

26. Bosch, *The OSRAM Ticket Manager: An Industry 4.0 app for Employees*, October 2017. Accessed August 27, 2018 at https://www.bosch-connected -industry.com/media/en/loesungen/nexeed_production_performance _manager/broschueren/case-study_osram_de_update201804.pdf.

27. Deborah Abrams Kaplan, "9 Trends in Last-Mile Delivery: How e-commerce Is Forcing Changes in How Retailers and Carriers Do Busi- ness," *SUPPLYCHAINDIVE*, May 22, 2017. Accessed June 11, 2018 at https://www .supplychaindive.com/news/last-mile-spotlight-trends-tech -gig-perfect/443091.

28. Sukh Dhillon, "Experiment, Launch, Iterate, Repeat: Why Product Develop- ment Is Never Complete," *Optimizely* (blog), September 6, 2017. Accessed June 11, 2018 at https://blog.optimizely.com/2017/09/06/experiment -launch-iterate-repeat.

Chapter 4

29. Aaron Pressman, "Why TaskRabbit's Gig Economy Model Is Thriving Under Ikea's Ownership," *Fortune*, July 17, 2018. Accessed October 29, 2018 at http://fortune.com/2018/07/17/taskrabbit-ikea-brown-philpot-undercover; "Flat-Rate IKEA® Furniture Assembly Is Now Available," *Community, TaskRabbit News* (blog), March 14, 2018. Accessed October 29, 2018 at https://blog.taskrabbit.com/2018/03/14/ikea-com-launch; Sonya Mann, "The Not-So-Obvious Reason IKEA Bought TaskRabbit," *Inc.com*, October 2, 2017. Accessed October 29, 2018 at https://www.inc.com/sonya-mann /ikea-taskrabbit-ethnography.html.

30. S. Colwell, M. Aung, V. Kanetkar, and A. Holden, "Toward a Measure of Service Convenience: Multi-Item Scale Development and Empirical Test," *Journal of Services Marketing* 22, no. 2 (2008): 160–169; J. Farquahr and J. Rowley, "Convenience: A Services Perspective," *Marketing Theory* 9, no. 4 (2009): 425–438.

31. SITA, "Boarding Pass Evolution," *Air Transport IT Review*, no. 3 (2014). Accessed September 3, 2018 at https://www.sita.aero/resources/air -transport-it-review/air-transport-it-review---issue-3-2014/boarding

-pass-evolution; "SITA History," SITA, 2018. Accessed September 3, 2018 at https://www.sita .aero/about-us/who-we-are/sita-history; "Who We Are," SITA, 2018. Accessed September 3, 2018 at https://www.sita.aero/about-us /who-we-are.

32. "About Us," Fandango, 2019. Accessed January 4, 2019 at https://www .fandango.com/AboutUs.aspx; "Help: Get Instant Answers: What is Mobile Ticket," Fandango, 2019. Accessed January 4, 2019 at https://www.fandango .com.

33. "About Netflix, Netflix Timeline," Netflix. Accessed October 29, 2018 at https://media.netflix.com/en/about-netflix.

34. Seatcraft, "Evolution of the Movie Theater Experience," *Seatcraft Home Theater* (blog), November 23, 2017. Accessed September 4, 2018 at https://www.seatcraft.com/evolution-of-the-movie-theater-experience; Jordan Kushins, "A Brief History of Sound in Cinema," *Popular Mechanics*, Febuary 24, 2016. Accessed September 5, 2018 at https:// www.popularme-chanics.com/culture/movies/a19566/a-brief-history-of-sound-in-cinema; Alexandre Bleus, "Immersive Sound Technologies," CinemaNext, c. 2018. Accessed September 5, 2018 at https:// www.cinemanext.com/features /showcases/immersive-sound-technologies; David Nield, "High-Resolution Cinema: 4K, 8K and Beyond," T3.com, February 10, 2017. Accessed September 5, 2018 at https://www.t3.com/news/high-resolution-cinema -4k-8k-and-beyond; Peter Suderman, "How Film Projection Got So Complicated—and How It Can Make or Break Your Movie Experience," Vox, March 6, 2017. Accessed September 4, 2018 at https://www.vox.com /culture/2017/3/6/14668690/film-formats-movie-projection; "Corporate Information," IMAX, 2018. Accessed September 4, 2018 at https://www .imax.com/content/corporate-information; "The Future of the Cinema Experience," Dasym, July 5, 2017. Accessed September 4, 2018 at https:// www.dasym .com/future-cinema-experience.

35. "About iRobot—Company Information," iRobot, 2018. Accessed October 30, 2018 at https://www.irobot.com/about-irobot/company-information; "Home Robots—Robot Vacuums," iRobot, 2018. Accessed October 29, 2018 at https://www.irobot.com/for-the-home/vacuuming/roomba.aspx; "About iRobot—Company Information—History," iRobot, 2018. Accessed October 30, 2018 at https://www.irobot.com/about-irobot/company-information /history.aspx; AmandaGal, "Still Doesn't Do Black Carpet," Amazon Cus-tomer Review, October 1, 2015. Accessed October 29, 2015 at https://www .amazon.com/gp/customer-reviews/R3T6QW0MUCQGLD/ref=cm_cr _arp_d_viewpnt?ie=UTF8&ASIN=B013E9L4ZS #R3T6QW0MUCQGLD; Victoria Song, "iRobot Roomba i7+," *PCMag*, October 25, 2018. Accessed October 29, 2018 at https://www.pcmag.com/review/364537/irobot -roomba-i7; Allie Volpe, "Should You Get a Robot Vacuum?" *New York*, May 11, 2018. Accessed October 30, 2018 at http://nymag.com/intelligencer /smarthome/should-you-get-a-robot-vacuum.html.

Chapter 5

36. For example, see Chandana Asif, Jiro Hiroaka, Tomas Jones, and Prerak Vohra, "Digitizing Customer Journeys and Processes: Stories from the Front Lines," in *McKinsey on Digital Services: Introducing the Next-Generation Operating Model*, McKinsey & Company, January 2017, pp. 50–57. Accessed September 11, 2018 at https://www.mckinsey.com/~/media/McKinsey /Business%20Functions/McKinsey%20Digital/Our%20Insights/Introducing %20the%20next-generation%20operating%20model/Introducing-the-next -gen-operating-model.ashx; Michael Hammer, "Reengineering Work: Don't Automate, Obliterate," *Harvard Business Review* 68, no. 4 (1990): 104–112; Art Kleiner, "Revisiting Reengineering," *strategy+business*, no. 20, July 1, 2000. Accessed September 13, 2018 at https://www.strategy-business.com /article/19570?gko=e05ea.

37. Asif et al., "Digitizing Customer Journeys and Processes."

38. Thomas W. Ferratt, "Collaborative Innovation with Information System and Functional Area Personnel" (presented to the Institute for Communication Technology Management, Marshall School of Business, University of Southern California, May 19, 2016, available at https://www.marshall.usc .edu/sites/default/files/2019-01/Collaborative%20Innovation-Ferratt%20R3 .pdf).

39. Ingmar Haffke, Bradley Kalgovas, and Alexander Benlian, "Options for Transforming the IT Function Using Bimodal IT," *MIS Quarterly Executive* 16, no. 2 (2017): 101–120.

40. Ann Majchrzak, Sabine Brunswicker, and Mehdi Bagherzadeh, "Open Innovation in U.S. Firms Today" (presented to the Institute for Communica- tion Technology Management, Marshall School of Business, University of Southern California, June 24, 2016, available at https://www.marshall.usc.edu /sites/default/files/2019-01/Open%20Innovation-Majchrzak%20R3.pdf).

41. "Fujitsu Forum 2018 Report, Special Session," Fujitsu, 2018. Accessed January 8, 2019 at http://www.fujitsu.com/global/vision/insights /201805event/index.html.

42. Marcelo Cano-Kollmann, Snehal Awate, T. J. Hannigan, and Ram Mudambi, "Burying the Hatchet for Catch-Up: Open Innovation among Industry Laggards in the Automotive Industry," *California Management Review* 60, no. 2 (2018): 17–42.

Chapter 6

43. Steven Zeitchik, "Netflix Was the Great Disruptor. Will It Now Be Dis- rupted?" *Washington Post*, July 17, 2018. Accessed September 18, 2018 at https://www.washingtonpost.com/business/2018/07/17/netflix-was-great -disruptor-is-it-about-be-disrupted-itself/?noredirect=on&utm_term =.430726a0b604.

44. Russell Davies, "Netflix Has Become the Envy of TV with So Much Data on Our Viewing Habits," *Campaign*, February 21, 2013. https://www.campaign-live.co.uk/article/netflix-become-envy-tv-so-data-viewing-habits/1171374

45. Edward Cone, "Eye in the Sky," *CIO Insight*, no. 72 (2006): 64–74.

46. Frank Nagle, "The Use and Security of Consumer Data" (presented to the Institute for Communication Technology Management, Marshall School of Business, University of Southern California, May 18, 2017, available at https://www.marshall.usc.edu/sites/default/files/2019-01/Customer%20 Data-Nagle%20R3.pdf).

47. Kif Leswing, "Apple Is Distancing Itself Again from Google and Facebook with a New Privacy Website," Business Insider, October 17, 2018. Accessed January 7, 2019 at https://www.businessinsider.com/apple-launches-new -privacy-website-and-method-to-delete-apple-id-2018-10; James Vincent, "Tim Cook Warns of 'Data-Industrial Complex' in Call for Comprehensive US Privacy Laws," The Verge, October 24, 2018. Accessed January 7, 2019 at https://www.theverge.com/2018/10/24/18017842/tim-cook-data-privacy -laws-us-speech-brussels; "Privacy: Our Approach to Privacy," Apple, 2019. Accessed January 7, 2019 at https://www.apple.com/privacy/approach-to -privacy.

48. Cheryl Wakslak, "Technology Use, Privacy Concern, and Employee Psychology" (presented to the Institute for Communication Technology Management, Marshall School of Business, University of Southern California, April 27, 2017, available at https://www.marshall.usc.edu/sites/default/files/2019 -01/Employee%20Privacy-Wakslak%20R3.pdf).

49. American Productivity & Quality Center, "Leveraging Knowledge Across the Value Chain: Caterpillar," *American Productivity & Quality Center Report*, 2006, pp. 103–114. Accessed February 4, 2018 at https://www.apqc.org /knowledge-base/documents/ leveraging-knowledge-across-value-chain-best-practices-report.

50. Thompson S. H. Teo, Rohit Nishant, Mark Goh, and Sameer Agarwal, "Leveraging Collaborative Technologies to Build a Knowledge Sharing Culture at HP Analytics," *MIS Quarterly Executive* 10, no. 1 (2011): 1–18.

51. Peter High, "The Future of Technology According to Bank of America's Chief Operations and Technology Officer," *Forbes*, June 19, 2017. Accessed September 21, 2018 at https://www.forbes.com/sites/peterhigh/2017/06/19 /the-future-of-technology-according-to-bank-of-americas-chief-operations -and-technology-officer/#2f2241e377c5.

52. Arif Ansari and Jinting Liu, "The Use of Analytics to Gain Competitive Advantages" (presented to the Institute for Communication Technology Management, Marshall School of Business, University of Southern California, June 23, 2017, available at https://www.marshall.usc.edu/sites/default /files/2019-01/Use%20of%20Analytics-Ansari%20R3.pdf).

53. For example, see Thomas H. Davenport, Jeanne G. Harris, David W. De Long, and Alvin L. Jacobson, "Data to Knowledge to Results: Building an

Analytic Capability," *California Management Review* 43, no. 2 (2001): 117–138; B. P. Watson, "Data Wrangling: How Procter and Gamble Maximizes Business Analytics," *CIO Insight*, January 30, 2012. Retrieved 10/31/2017 from http://www.cioinsight.com/c/a/Business-Intelligence /Data-Wrangling-How-PG-Maximizes-Business-Analytics-782673; B. H. Wixom, H. J. Watson, and T. Werner, "Developing an Enterprise Business Intelligence Capability: The Norfolk Southern Journey," *MIS Quarterly Executive* 10, no. 2 (2011): 61–71.

Chapter 7

54. "Brands—Zillow," Zillow Group, 2018. Accessed October 25, 2018 at https://www.zillowgroup.com/zillow; "About Zillow Group," Zillow Group, 2018. Accessed October 25, 2018 at https://www.zillowgroup.com/about -zillow-group.

55. "Zestimate," Zillow, 2006–2018. Accessed October 25, 2018 at https://www .zillow.com/zestimate; "Calculating Your Zestimate—and How You Can Influence It," Zillow, 2006–2018. Accessed October 25, 2018 at https://www .zillow.com/sellers-guide/influencing-your-zestimate; Jay Thompson, "Homeowners Can Now Make Instant Updates to Zestimates," *Premier Agent* (blog), February 27, 2015. Accessed October 25, 2018 at https://www.zillow .com/agent-resources/blog/make-instant-updates-to-zestimate.

56. "Steris Healthcare Services," Up! Your Service, c. 2018. Accessed September 29, 2018 at https://www.upyourservice.com/proven-results/customer -success/steris-healthcare-services.

57. Degordian, 2019, https://www.degordian.com. Accessed January 9, 2019; Daniel Ackermann, "How We Handled Rapid Growth & Maintained Our Culture," *Education Hub* (Degordian blog), December 22, 2014. Accessed January 9, 2019 at https://www.degordian.com/education/blog/handled -rapid-growth-maintained-culture.

58. Peter Cardon, "Leadership Communication on Internal Digital Platforms: Driving Better Culture and Stronger Performance" (presented to the Institute for Communication Technology Management, Marshall School of Business, University of Southern California, April 18, 2016, available at https://www.marshall.usc.edu/sites/default/files/2019-01/Leadership%20 Communication-Cardon%20R3.pdf). There is also an article based on the study: Peter W. Cardon, Yumi Huang, and Gerard Power, "Leadership Communication on Internal Digital Platforms, Emotional Capital, and Corporate Performance: The Case for Leader-Centric Listening," *International Journal of Business Communication*, published online February 6, 2019, at https://doi.org/10.1177/2329488419828808.

59. Quy Huy, and Andrew Shipilov, "The Key to Social Media Success within Organizations," *MIT Sloan Management Review* 54, no. 1 (2012): 73–81.

60. Neil Siegel, "Geographically-Distributed Engineering" (presented to the Institute for Communication Technology Management, Marshall School of

Business, University of Southern California, 2017, available at https://www
.marshall.usc.edu/sites/default/files/2019-01/Distributed%20Engineering
-Siegel%20R3.pdf).

61. Anonymous, "Design Reviews," c. 2018. Accessed October 2, 2018 at
http://people.ucalgary.ca/~design/engg251/First%20Year%20Files/design
_reviews.pdf.

Chapter 8

62. "Connecting the World," FedEx. Accessed October 30, 2018 at https://about
.van.fedex.com/wp-content/uploads/2014/10/FX_Corp _Brochure2017.pdf.

63. James Henderson, "Interview: FedEx and Exporting in the Digitised Era,"
Supply Chain Digital, April 10, 2018. Accessed October 30, 2018 at https://
www.supplychaindigital.com/logistics/interview-fedex-and-exporting
-digitised-era.

64. For example, see Christopher Koch, "The ABCs of ERP," 2002. Accessed
October 9, 2018 at http://wikifab.dimf.etsii.upm.es/wikifab/images/d/da
/The_ABCs_of_ERP.pdf; Michael Nadeau, "ERP Heads for the CLOUD,"
CIO, September 20, 2016, pp. 7–15; Abrar Ullah; Rohaizat Bin Baharun;
Khalil Nor, MD; Muhammad Siddique; and Mansoor Nazir Bhatti, "Enter-
prise Resource Planning (ERP) Systems and ERP Quality Factors: A Litera-
ture Review," *Journal of Managerial Sciences* 11 (2017): 297–322.

65. Nick Vyas and Cecilia Ledesma, "The Future Outlook of Supply Chain
Management" (presented to the Institute for Communication Technology
Management, Marshall School of Business, University of Southern California, July 6, 2017, available at https://www.marshall.usc.edu/sites/default
/files/2019-01/Supply%20Chain-Vyas%20R3.pdf).

66. Oxford Economics, *Future Trends and Market Opportunities in the World's
Largest 750 Cities*, c. 2013. Retrieved March 1, 2018 from https://www
.oxfordeconomics.com/Media/Default/landing-pages/cities/OE-cities
-summary.pdf; Yuval Atsmon, Peter Child, Richard Dobbs, and Laxman
Narasimhan, "Winning the $30 Trillion Decathlon: Going for Gold in
Emerging Markets," *McKinsey Quarterly*, no. 4 (2012): 20–35. Retrieved
March 1, 2018 from https://www.mckinsey.com/business-functions
/strategy-and-corporate-finance/our-insights/winning-the-30-trillion
-decathlon-going-for-gold-in-emerging-markets.

67. Neal Karlinsky, "Judge a Toy By Its Box—How Amazon and Hasbro Came
Together to Invent Better Packaging," *Day One* (Amazon blog), July 20, 2018.
Accessed January 10, 2019 at https://blog.aboutamazon.com/sustainability
/judge-a-toy-by-its-box.

68. Edgar H. Schein, "What You Need to Know About Organizational Culture,"
Training & Development Journal 40, no. 1 (1986): 30–33.

69. Wendy L. Ulrich, "HRM and Culture: History, Ritual, and Myth," *Human
Resource Management* 23, no. 2 (1984): 117–128.

70. Jonathan Schanz and Christine De Lille, "Customer Experience Strategy Turned into Hands? On Actions Through a Design Approach," *Design Management Journal* 12, no. 1 (2017): 28–39.

71. Bernard Marr, "Internet of Things and Predictive Maintenance Transform the Service Industry," *Forbes*, May 5, 2017. Accessed January 10, 2019 at https://www.forbes.com/sites/bernardmarr/2017/05/05/internet-of-things -and-predictive-maintenance-transform-the-service-industry/#1b7e2b47eaf4.

72. California Fuel Cell Partnership, *A California Road Map: The Commercialization of Hydrogen Fuel Cell Vehicles*, June 2012, retrieved March 14, 2018 from https://cafcp.org/sites/default/files/A%20California%20Road%20 Map %20June%202012%20%28CaFCP%20technical%20version%29.pdf; David Undercoffler, "Here Come the Hydrogen Stations," *Automotive News*, vol. 90, no. 6727 (May 30, 2016), retrieved 3/14/2018 from http://www .autonews.com/article/20160530/OEM06/305309986/here-come-the -hydrogen-stations.

73. Lars Perner, "Crossing the Road Toward Innovation: Identifying and Addressing Chicken-and-Egg Problems" (presented to the Institute for Communication Technology Management, Marshall School of Business, University of Southern California, June 8, 2017, available at https:// www. marshall.usc.edu/sites/default/files/2019-01/Chicken%20Egg-Perner%20R3 .pdf); Kyle Mayer, "Managing Technical Partners in a Networked Age" (presented to the Institute for Communication Technology Management, Marshall School of Business, University of Southern California, June 10, 2016, available at https://www.marshall.usc.edu/sites/default/files/2019-01 /Managing%20Partners-Mayer%20R3.pdf).

Conclusion

74. Joel Lee, "Waze vs. Google Maps: Which App Will Navigate Home Faster," MakeUseOf, May 5, 2017. Accessed October 17, 2018 at https://www .makeuseof.com/tag/wave-vs-google-maps.

75. Rob Nightingale, "How Does Google Maps Work?" MakeUseOf, January 8, 2017. Accessed October 17, 2018 at https://www.makeuseof.com/tag /technology-explained-google-maps-work.

Acknowledgments

We recognize and appreciate the work and support of many who have made this book possible. The first opportunity for us to work together occurred while Tom was on sabbatical from the University of Dayton in 2015. Sabbatical support came from Department Chair Jay Prasad, Dean Paul Bobrowski, and Provost Paul Benson at the University of Dayton. While on sabbatical, Tom was a visiting scholar at the University of Southern California (USC), thanks to the support of Ann Majchrzak, Omar El Sawy, and their department chair, Yehuda Bassok, of the Marshall School of Business at USC. We also wish to thank Dean Jim Ellis, Marshall School of Business at USC, and Dean John Mittelstaedt, School of Business Administration at the University of Dayton, for their support.

The Marshall School of Business is the home of the Institute for Communication Technology Management (CTM), a consortium-funded think tank dedicated to understanding how technology is changing our view of business and how business is guiding the way technology drives changes to markets. As director of CTM, Jerry constructed a series of linked research projects from 2015 to 2017 designed to shed new light on the technology-driven changes that are redefining a company's culture and behaviors of their served markets. With the support of Dean Ellis and the USC Marshall CTM members, a group of faculty experts were assembled to focus on a piece of a much larger puzzle.

As a visiting scholar, Tom was responsible for one of those projects and worked with Jerry to compile the components into a more cohesive story, but we would not have been able to write this book without key contributions from the expert researchers responsible for the CTM projects. That work, which we reference throughout the book, helped us develop insights related to the real-time revolution. We wish to pay tribute and acknowledge the substantial contributions made by USC as a whole and to several key contributors specifically.

- Arif Ansari is a professor of clinical data sciences and operations at USC-Marshall as well as an expert in the area of data mining, business intelligence, data warehousing, and intelligent systems and technologies, a field in which he has fifteen years of research experience. He has published in *IEEE Transactions on Systems, Man, and Cybernetics*. Professor Ansari received Marshall's Golden Apple Award in 2006.

- Mehdi Bagherzadeh is an assistant professor of innovation management in the Department of Strategy and Entrepreneurship at NEOMA Business School, France. He is also a research fellow at the Research Center for Open Digital Innovation (RCODI), Purdue University. Mehdi was a visiting PhD student at the Marshall School of Business and at RCODI between December 2014 and September 2015. His research revolves around governance dynamics of open and collaborative innovation projects and its effect on innovation performance.

- Sabine Brunswicker is an associate professor at Purdue University and is an internationally recognized scholar with a particular interest in open digital innovation, describing new ways of using information technologies to organize the collective design and use of innovative digital goods. She is also the founder and director of the Research Center for Open Digital Innovation (RCODI) and an adjunct professor of digital innovation in the School of Information Systems at Queensland University of Technology, Brisbane, Australia. Sabine is a computational social scientist, bridging social science and computing when studying open digital innovation. Her interests include open-source software communities, civic crowdsourcing, open data app competitions, collective software design and reuse, and collective energy conservation through interactive home-energy monitoring applications and visualizations.

- Pete Cardon is the academic director for the MBA Program for Professionals and Managers and a professor of clinical business communications at USC-Marshall, where he teaches a variety of business communication courses. He researches team communication, the role of technology in leadership communication, and intercultural business communication. Professor Cardon previously served as president of the Association for Business Communication. Before working in higher education, he held several marketing and management positions in the tourism and manufacturing industries where, along the way, he has worked in China for three years and traveled to approximately fifty countries for work and research. He is also the author of *Business Communication: Developing Leaders for a Networked World.*

- Omar El Sawy is the Kenneth King Stonier Professor of Business Administration and professor of data sciences and operations at USC-Marshall. His expertise is in digital business strategy in dynamic environments and business models for digital platforms. He served as director of research for Marshall's Institute for Communication Technology Management from 2001 to 2007 and is the author of over one hundred papers. A seven-time winner of the Society for Information Management's annual academic paper award, he is currently senior editor of *MIS Quarterly* and on several editorial boards. He has served as advisor to the United Nations Development Programme in Egypt and as a Fulbright Scholar in Finland.

- Ann Majchrzak is a professor of data sciences and operations and associates chair in business administration at USC-Marshall. She teaches digital innovation and holds concurrent appointments as a visiting professor at ESADE Business School, Ramon Llull University, Barcelona, and at LUISS, Rome School of Business and Management, in the areas of innovation and organization. She is also an external expert for the Information Systems and Innovation Faculty Research Group in the Department of Management at the London School of Economics.

- Kyle Mayer is a professor of management and organization at USC-Marshall with a research interest in understanding how firms govern relationships with other firms, with particular attention to the contract and its role in establishing a framework for the relationship. His research has been published in *Organization Science, Academy of Management Journal, Management Science,* and *Journal of Law, Economics, and Organization.* He served on the editorial boards of *Academy of Management Journal, Organization Science, Academy of Management Review,* and *Strategic Management Journal.* He received a Golden Apple Award in 2003, Marshall's Educator of the Year Award in 2006, and a Mellon Mentoring Award from USC in 2006.

- Frank Nagle is an assistant professor in the Strategy Unit at Harvard Business School. There, he studies the economics of IT and digitization with a focus on the value of crowdsourcing, and how these topics relate to the future of work. His research interests include free digital goods, cybersecurity, and generating strategic predictions from unstructured big data. His work utilizes large data sets derived from online social networks, financial market information, and surveys of enterprise IT usage. He currently advises the OECD Working Group on Innovation and Technology Policy and has consulted for the World Bank, the US Treasury Department, the Social Security Administration, and various companies in the technology, defense, and energy sectors. Prior to joining HBS, he was an assistant professor in the Management and Organization Department at the Marshall School of Business.

- Lars Perner is an assistant professor of clinical marketing at USC-Marshall, where his research interests focus on nonprofit marketing, sponsored fund-raising, consumer behavior, consumer price response, branding, and bargain hunting. His work has been published in the *Journal of Marketing Management, Journal of Marketing Education, Journal of Consumer Affairs,* and *Journal of Consumer Psychology.* He currently serves as a faculty coordinator for the Department of Marketing's undergraduate introductory marketing course sections, which serve approximately 1,600 students every academic year.

- Pernille Rydén is head of studies and an associate professor at the Technical University of Denmark and lecturer, Copenhagen Business School, Department of Marketing. Pernille is a mindset specialist, an executive trainer (EMBA and coach/facilitator), author, and public speaker. Her work in the areas of strategic cognition, management, and customer-focused digital transformation provides well-founded practical as well as disruptive solutions to management challenges of tomorrow's enterprises. She is also ambassador of the Academy of Management's Managerial and Organizational Cognition Division.

- Neil Siegel is the IBM Professor of Engineering Management and professor of industrial and systems engineering practice at USC-Viterbi. His personal research contributions have centered around the systems engineering problem of developing large, complex (both technically and social) societal systems. He has been the actual lead designer and/or program manager for several such systems and has drawn from those experiences to create new insights into the root cause of process failures with a set of novel techniques that provide better outcomes for such programs. He has also sponsored important research in the field of human-computer interaction.

- Nick Vyas is the founding executive director of the USC-Marshall Center for Global Supply Chain Management and academic director for the Master of Science in Global Supply Chain Management program. As an assistant professor of clinical data sciences and operations, Nick is educating the next generation of business leaders. He is a specialist in operation excellence using digital transformation and an expert in global supply chain management (GSCM) at USC-Marshall. Nick has implemented large-scale enterprise-wide transformation projects for over four hundred projects globally that have increased efficiency for clients in the fields of health care, service, military, retail, and end-to-end supply chain.

- Cheryl Wakslak is an associate professor of management and organization at USC-Marshall. Her research focuses on basic questions of cognition and interpersonal connection, establishing the way that people use different styles of thinking to help them connect with those closer to them and those farther away. In much of this work she explores the role of abstraction in facilitating connections across distance. She uses these insights to look at a range of organizationally relevant outcomes, including communication, learning, leadership, venture capital investment, and decision making. Her findings have been published in numerous scholarly outlets, including top journals in management, marketing, and psychology.

- Yumi Huang is a versatile and capable researcher who provided a great deal of assistance to the entire team and kept everyone on track.

- Cecilia Ledesma is a graduate student of the Master of Science in Global Supply Chain Management program at USC who aided in our understanding of the future of supply chain ecosystems.

- Jinting Liu is a PhD candidate in applied mathematics at USC who helped us understand how companies are using analytics.

We especially would like to express our gratitude to Ann Majchrzak, Omar El Sawy, and Pernille Rydén, who provided the inspiration and encouragement we needed to tackle such a complicated topic. Steve Piersanti, our editor with Berrett-Koehler Publishers, helped us shape our theme into the real-time revolution. We also wish to express our thanks to Ed Lawler III, director of the Center for Effective Organizations (CEO) in the Marshall School of Business at USC, for introducing us to Steve.

Throughout the book we have cited numerous published sources that provided examples of real-time organizations and relevant references. We express our gratitude to all of these authors, organizations, and sources.

Converting our initial draft to a published book has involved the work of many people. We are thankful to all of them. For example, they include the reviewers who provided feedback on our initial draft and the artist who designed the cover. They also include all the staff of Berrett-Koehler Publishers who worked on this book.

A special note of thanks is extended to the CTM member companies that include AT&T, Children's Hospital of Los Angeles, the City of Los Angeles, Telus, Verizon, CenturyLink, TDS, Warner Bros., and 20th Century Fox. Special thanks are due to Chris Sambar, Dave Abbott, Liz Huszarik, Gnanasekaran Swaminathan, Ibrahim Gedeon, John Devine, Joe Hanley, Justin Hertz, Lani Ingram, Pam Allison, Peter Taft, Steve Garske, and Will Somers.

We ask forgiveness from those we have not specifically thanked here that we should have.

Index

Note: Locators followed by the italicized letter "*f*" indicate a figure on that page.

About the Authors

 **Jerry Power** is the executive director of the Institute for Communication Technology Management (CTM) at University of Southern California's (USC) Marshall School of Business. CTM and its board of corporate leaders are actively engaged in identifying emerging trends driven by the rapid evolution of digital communications technologies and services. Through its research and educational programs, the institute explores the new opportunities and challenges for the business community in the age of automation, mobility, broadband, and digital content. CTM embraces the increasingly dynamic nature of the market and harnesses the thought leadership of academia to link them with issues facing government and corporate organizations. The ultimate goal of CTM is to find new ways for these organizations to thrive as they serve the emerging needs of customers and citizens in an evolving business climate. Jerry is also a founding member of the Intelligent IoT Integrator (I3) Consortium. I3 is a private-public-academic group of partnered entities working to create an open-source framework that supports a democratized (IoT) marketplace. By supporting the creation of diverse communities of independent IoT device owners, participants in the emerging data economy are able to reduce the friction associated with deploying and operating in an information-rich environment. The consortium recognizes the importance and the personalized nature of privacy, trust, and incentives as key enablers of a sustainable, managed, and networked IoT infrastructure that supports collaborative IoT environments. By removing the IoT market inhibitors, the complexities associated with value creation from IoT data streams are reduced, thereby supporting the ongoing development of the market. Prior to his time at USC, Jerry spent more than thirty years working for Alcatel-Lucent and Siemens, where he was engaged in developing and supporting products and concepts that shaped the structure and use of modern digital networking systems.

Tom Ferratt has had a distinguished career, primarily as a university professor. He has been an author, teacher, researcher, and consultant. Most of his work has focused on management information systems (MIS). The Advanced Practices Council of the Society for Information Management, a professional network for information technology (IT) leadership, has sponsored his work on developing and retaining a world-class IT staff. That work led to his first book, *Coping with Labor Scarcity in Information Technology: Strategies and Practices for Effective Recruitment and Retention.* Other work with chief information officers includes developing a community health information network with hospitals in the Greater Dayton Area Hospital Association to share patient information across emergency rooms. Tom's research has been published and featured in leading publications, including *MIS Quarterly, Information Systems Research, Academy of Management Journal, Communications of the ACM* (Association for Computing Machinery), and *Computerworld.* He has been on the editorial boards of internationally recognized IT journals and has served in leadership roles with the Special Interest Group on Computer Personnel Research and, subsequent to its merger, the Special Interest Group on Management Information Systems of the Association for Computing Machinery. He is currently professor emeritus at the University of Dayton, where he served as the Sherman-Standard Register Endowed Chair in MIS and as an associate dean in the School of Business Administration. His undergraduate degree is from the University of Notre Dame, and his MBA and PhD in business administration are from Ohio State University. He was a member of the faculty and a department chair at Drake University and a visiting professor at Indiana University. He and Jerry Power met while Tom was a visiting scholar at the USC in 2015. Their work together eventually led to collaborating on this book.

Dear reader,

Thank you for picking up this book and welcome to the worldwide BK community! You're joining a special group of people who have come together to create positive change in their lives, organizations, and communities.

What's BK all about?

Our mission is to connect people and ideas to create a world that works for all.

Why? Our communities, organizations, and lives get bogged down by old paradigms of self-interest, exclusion, hierarchy, and privilege. But we believe that can change. That's why we seek the leading experts on these challenges—and share their actionable ideas with you.

A welcome gift

To help you get started, we'd like to offer you a **free copy** of one of our bestselling ebooks:

www.bkconnection.com/welcome

When you claim your **free ebook**, you'll also be subscribed to our blog.

Our freshest insights

Access the best new tools and ideas for leaders at all levels on our blog at ideas.bkconnection.com.

Sincerely,

Your friends at Berrett-Koehler

Certified

Corporation